A JUDGMENT THEORY

A Theory of Cognition, Cultures,
Language, and Contracts

DR. AHMED RIAHI-BELKAOUI

A judgment made by Freud:

"...I have found little that is "good" about human beings on the whole. In my experience most of them are trash, no matter whether they publicly subscribe to this or that ethical doctrine or none at all....If we are to talk of ethics, I subscribe to a high ideal from which most of the human beings I have come across depart most lamentably"

Freud, S., Psychoanalysis and Faith: Dialogues with the Reverend Oscar Pfister (New York: Basic Books, 1963), pp. 61-62.

ISBN: 1475284667

ISBN 13:   9781475284669

Contents

Preface:
A General Judgment Theory

There is a definite need for a better understanding of what takes place when individuals from any culture form judgments and make decisions when faced a relevant phenomena. The theory proposed in this book rests on a judgment/decision model. This model assumes that cognition guides the judgment/decision process and that the schemata underlying this cognitive process are in turn shaped by national culture, language, organizational culture, and contractual agreements. The model is essentially a relativism model whereby the judgment/decision process is assumed to be determined by cognitive, cultural, linguistic, organizational, and contractual factors. An appreciation of these relativisms and of the final theory is fundamental to an understanding of the judgment/decision process.

This book provides a thorough examination of each of the five relativisms affecting the judgment/decision process as well as the theory that builds on these relativisms. It provides guidance to the researcher and practitioner alike in their search for and testing of competing hypotheses to explain the judgment/decision process. The judgment/decision process is rich and complex, as illustrated by a spectrum of theoretically and empirically based relativisms.

The book consists of five chapters that deal, in turn, with cognitive, cultural, linguistic, organizational, and contractual relativism in accounting. Each chapter examines the theory and findings underlying these relativisms in the social sciences and their contribution to explaining the judgment/decision process. The final chapter looks toward the possibility of a general theory. The book may be used as a guide to the understanding and researching of the thought processes underlying the judgment/decision process.

Cognitive Relativism

Introduction

What happens when people make decisions about a phenomenon, amid the pressures, constraints, dangers, and opportunities of today's environment?[1] This chapter presents a model which focuses on the cognitive processes employed by a decision maker attempting to use his/her judgment to make a decision about a phenomenon. Basically, both judgment and decision are the products of a set of social cognitive operations that include the observation of information on the phenomenon and the formation of a schema to represent the phenomenon that is stored in memory and later retrieved when needed to allow the formation of a judgment and a decision. Before presenting the model an elaboration on the notion and use of schemata in cognitive psychology is necessary.

Schemata In Cognitive Psychology

The Notion of Schema-Guided Processes

The schema theory as developed by F.C. Barlett[2] served as the stimulus for all schema theories. As defined by Barlett, a schema is "an active organization of past reactions, or past experiences, which must always be supposed to be operating in any well-adapted organic response."[3] They are complex unconscious knowledge, as "masses of organized past experiences."[4] They are generic cognitive representations, in the sense that they constitute a process that can deal with an indefinitely large number of new instances.

Modern views of schemata refer generally to cognitive structures that represent organized knowledge about a given concept or a given stimulus and that serve as mechanisms for the interaction of old knowledge and new knowledge in perception, language, thought, and memory.

Schemata are generally regarded as fundamental elements upon which all information processing depends. They constitute a theory about knowledge: how knowledge is represented, and how that representation facilitates the use of knowledge in numerous ways. As stated by D. E. Rumelhart, "schemata are employed in the process of interpreting sensory data, in retrieving information from memory, in organizing actions, in the determining of goals and sub-goals, in the allocation of resources and generally in guiding the flow of processing in the system."[5] In fact, useful analyses of schemata suggested by Rumelhart include plays, theories, procedures, and parsers.[6] Properties of schemas include the following:

1. A schema represents a prototypical abstraction of the complex concept it represents.

2. A schema is induced from past experiences with numerous exemplars of the complex concept it represents.

3. A schema can guide the organization of incoming information into clusters of knowledge that are "instantiations" of the schema itself.

4. When one of the constituent concepts of a schema is missing in the input, its features can be inferred from default values" in the schema.[7]

Schemata versus Categories

Jean Randler made an unusual distinction between two types of representations categories and schemata. Categories are denoted by verbal or nonverbal symbols (i.e., "names") and are represented by a set of features that serve as the basis for inferring membership in it. Schemata, on the other hand, are cognitive representations whose features, like those of categories, are organized according to specific a priori spatial, temporal, or logical criteria.[8] Categories and schemata function differently. As Robert S. Wyer and S.E. Gordon note:

Information about a set of attributes processed by the members of a particular category may not spontaneously activate this category unless either (a) the attributes are very strongly and uniquely associated with it, (b) one has a specific objective that leads the object being described to be classified, or (c) a category and its characteristic features are already activated at the time the information is received... In contrast, information that describes the characteristic features of a schema may become more inclined to activate the schema spontaneously.[9]

Schema Growth and Change

In considering schema growth and change the evidence favors a perseverance effect whereby generic schemata are resistant to change even in the face of contrary evidence.[10] In fact, people may even interpret exceptions as proving a given schema,[11] unless they are asked to counterargue it, to explain why their favorite theory might be wrong.[12]

Schemata are developed from experience with instances of the category in question and become more complex, more abstract, and more organized with experience. With increasing experience a schema becomes more mature and more complex. Hence, the schemata of experts contain more informational elements than those of novices, are more organized, contain more links, and may have a more complex hierarchy.[13-15]

Sources of Activation for Schemas

D.G. Bobrow and D.A. Norman distinguish between two basic sources of activation for schemata: conceptually driven and data-driven processing.[16] In conceptually driven processing, an activated schema in turn activates a subschemata with the expectation that this will account for some portion of the input data. In data-driven processing, the activated subschema causes the activation of the various schemas of which it is a component. Data-driven processing goes from part to the whole. In another source of activation, known as schema-directed processing, the activation is assumed to go in both directions. It proceeds as follows:

Some events occur at the sensory system. The occurrence of this event "automatically activates certain low level" schemata (much schemata might be called *"feature detectors"*). The low level schemata, in turn, activates (in a data driven fashion) certain of the "higher level" schemata (the most probable ones) of which they are constituents. These "higher level" schemata then initiate conceptually driven processing by activating the subschemata not already activated in an attempt to evaluate their goodness of fit.[17]

Encoding of Information in a Schema

For W.F. Brewer and G.V. Nakamura, the interaction of old knowledge with new knowledge involves two processes: one refers to the modification of the generic knowledge in the relevant schema, while the other refers to the construction of a specified instantiated memory representation, where the instantiated schema is the cognitive structure that results from the interaction of the old information and the new information from the episodic unit.[18]

The encoding of information is in fact subject to at least two interpretations. First, the interpretation proposed by R. S. Woodswork and H. Schlosberg[19] postulates that once a schema is activated by incoming episodic information, features that are inconsistent with the implications of this schema are appended to the representation of information as "corrections." A second conceptualization proposed by A. C. Graesser, S.E. Gordon, and J.D. Sawyer,[20] known as the "script-pointer-plus-tag formulation, postulates that when people receive information that is interpretable in terms of a prototypic event schema (script), they do not retain the information itself but a "pointer" to the general script, along with an indication of the values of the information that instantiate the script variables. If features of the information do not match attributes of the generic script, and thus cannot be reconstructed, they are appended to the representations as "tag." Basically, new information is represented by a series of "pointer" to prototypic event schemata that can be used to understand or describe the event, accompanied when necessary by "tags" denoting objects or events that cannot be derived from the event schemata alone.

Social Schema Research

Social schema research investigates self-schemata, person schemata, script or event schemata, and person-in-situation schemata.[21]

The self-schema contains cognitive generalizations about the self that are derived from past experiences. People are generally self-schematic on dimensions that are of importance to them, on which they perceive themselves as extreme, and on which they perceive the opposite to be untrue.[22] They are schematic on those dimensions perceived to be of lesser importance to them.

Research on perception shows that people who are schematic on a particular dimension recognize and filter rapidly incoming information about the dimension, notice the dimension in other people, and think harder about kinds of schema-relevant information.[23]

Research on memory shows that self-schematic people remember schema-relevant information, are difficult to change, have more accessible knowledge about others because of the sheer familiarity of self-knowledge, and are more affect-laden in knowledge about others, especially unfamiliar individuals.[24,25]

Research on inference shows that people make rapid predictions about their own behavior that are consistent with their self-schemata.[26] Under certain circumstances these predictions take longer than for aschematics,[27] especially if the judgment is novel.

The person-schema contains cognitive generalizations about trait and behavior information common to certain groups or types of people.

Research on perception shows that categories for people, like categories for objects, are organized hierarchically.[28] Research on memory shows that schemata for people's traits and goals typically help the perceiver to remember schema-consistent information in more detail than would be possible without the schemata. Research on inference shows that person schemata affect subsequent inferences.

The evidence on person schemata is summarized as follows:

Person schemata include protypical representations of traits such as extroversion and introversion, as well as notions of what behavior is consistent with a given goal. Person schemata of all sorts shape the processes of perception, memory, and inference to conform to our general assumptions about other people. The effects of schemata on perception, memory and inference are not necessarily well suited to accuracy in identifying individual instances. Schemata are used by the mind to manage such processes economically, if not accurately.29

The script or event schema contains cognitive generalizations that describe the appropriate sequence of events in a given situation.[30] Research on script or event schemata is summarized as follows:

Script or event schema describe sequences of activity from everyday life. They contain props, roles and sequence rules. Scripts also may be subdivided into segments (scenes). Like other schemata, scripts guide the perception of ambiguous information and often shape memory toward schema consistent information. Inferences can be seen as filling in gaps where information was missing, and gap filling appears to be exaggerated by repeated encounters with the script. Most of the functions of scripts echo those of other schemata, in their focus on relevant and usually on consistent information in perception, memory and inference.[31]

The person-in-situation or role schema contains cognitive generalizations about people in situations or scripts for behavior in situations. Role schemata not only help perception, memory, and inference but may be a way to account for stereotyping.

Research on perception shows that categorization instantiates the stereotypic content of the schema whether or not the person fits the category and in the process minimizes the amount of variability and complexity that may exitst in the category.[32,33] In addition to minimizing variability and complexity, a schema slants perception of the content of what a person does.

Research on memory shows that the role schema shapes memory in a schema-consistent fashion. In addition, the categorical information seems to override the details of the specific instance.[34] Schema-discrepant information is, however, likely to receive added attention at input, if task conditions allow. Attentional processes can facilitate re-membering inconsistent information.[35]

A Congnitive View Of The Judgment/Decision Process

In what follows a model of the judgment/decision process is proposed as an exercise in social perception and cognition, requiring both formal and implicit judgment.[36] The primary input to this process is a problem or phenomenon that needs to be solved and requires a judgment preceding either a preference or a decision. The model consists of the following steps:

1. Observation of the phenomenon by the decision maker
2. Schema formation or building of the phenomenon
3. Schema organization or storage
4. Attention and recognition process triggered by a stimulus
5. Retrieval of stored information needed for the judgment decision
6. Reconsideration and integration of retrieved information with new information
7. Judgment process
8. Decision/action response

Observation of the Phenomenon by the Decision Maker

The decision maker is assumed to have the opportunity to observe the phenomenon. To understand the phenomenon, the decision maker may be given some information which is deemed diagnostic. If this information is not provided, the decision maker may seek the information and test available information judged most relevant to the phenomenon. Following H.H. Kelly's approach to causal attribution,[37] the search behavior may concentrate on these types of available information:

1. *Consensus information:* how this phenomenon and other phenomena were rated or performed on given dimensions
2. *Distinctiveness information:* how this phenomenon was rated or performed on various other dimensions
3. *Consistency information:* how this phenomenon was rated or performed on important dimensions in the past

Evidence shows that subjects tend to focus more on distinctiveness or consistency information than on consensus information.[38]

The search behavior is not misguided. It is fair to assume that the decision maker has some expectations about the phenomenon which may determine the type of information sought. These expectations are termed *preconceived notions* in A. S. De Nisi et al.'s model.[39] They result from the decision maker's previous experiences with the phenomenon. These expectations or preconceived notions may bias the decision maker toward choosing some information rather than other information. Providing background information prior to observation contributes to this phenomenon.[40,41] R. S. Wyer and T. K. Srull maintain that prior information predisposes the subject to select one of a number of frames of references.[42] Bias is a result of the tendency to seek evidence confirming preconceived notions rather than neutral or disconfirming evidence.[43-45]

Schema Formation or Building

Once the phenomenon has been observed, the relevant information is encoded in the sense that it is categorized on the basis of experience and organized in memory along schemata or knowledge structures. As put by R. E. Nisbett and L. Ross:

Few, if any, stimuli are approached for the first time by the adult. Instead, they are processed through pre-existing systems of schematized and abstracted knowledge-beliefs, theories, propositions and schemas. These knowledge structures label and categorized objects and events quickly and, for the most part, accurately. They also define a set of expectations about objects and events and suggest appropriate responses to them.[46]

A schema can be simply an update of templates that existed prior to the occurrence of a known phenomenon or a new template generated by the occurrence of a new phenomenon. In the first case, little ambiguity is assumed to exist and therefore the encoding follows an automatic process.[47] In the second case, no immediate available schema exists, and a controlled categorization process is triggered to determine which schema is consistent with the dimensions of the phenomenon. Both processes are suggested in the case of the encoding of information or performance appraisal:

Thus, both the automatic and controlled processes have the same end result: the assignment of a person to a category based on prototype-matching process. The difference is whether the stimulus person's behavior is sufficiently consistent with other cues to allow the categorization to proceed automatically or whether a controlled process must be used to determine which category is consistent with the individual's behavior. The actual category assignment is a function of contextual factors influencing the salience of particular categories and stimulus characteristics, as well as individual differences among perceivers that render some categories and their prototypes more available than others and some stimulus features more salient than others.48

Basically, a phenomenon may be categorized in a given schema, by virtue of its possession of obvious or salient attributes known to the perceiver. When no salient category prototype or schema provides a natural framework, the automatic process is superseded by a controlled process or a consciously monitored process.[49]

The controlled process can be triggered by either a new phenomenon or new features of a known phenomenon that are inconsistent with a previous categorization. In the latter case a recategorization is invoked until the inconsistency is resolved and a new schema is used to describe the phenomenon, causing a reconstruction of memories about the phenomenon such that memories consistent with the new categorization are more available.

Schema Organization and Storage

After information about a given phenomenon is encoded to form a representation or schema, it is stored and maintained in long-term memory. E. Tulving distinguishes between episodic and semantic memory.[50] Basically, a person's episodic memories are personal while semantic memory is knowledge of words and symbols, their meanings and referent knowledge of the relations among words, and the rules or algorithms for manipulating words, symbols and the relations among them. R. C. Atkinson and R. M. Shiffrin maintain that the basic structural features of episodic memory are three memory stores: the sensory register, the short-term store, and the long-term store.[51] Information enters the memory system through the various senses and goes first to the sensory register whose function is to preserve incoming information long enough for it to be selectively transmitted into the memory system. It is kept there less than a second and is lost either through decay or erasure by overwriting.

The information then goes to the short-term store, "working in memory" where conscious mental processes are performed. It is where consciousness exercises its function. Information can be kept indefinitely here provided that it is given constant attention; if not, it is lost through decay in twenty to thirty seconds.

The information next goes to the long-term store through a conscious or unconscious process where it can be held indefinitely and often permanently (although it can be lost due to decay or interference of various sorts). The long-term store is assumed to have unlimited capacity. In this multistore model information about the phenomenon moves through different and separate memory systems, ending with a long-term store where semantic information is maintained along meaning-based codes or schemata. It is important to realize at this stage that if the person intends to remember the phenomenon for all time, he/she must perform a different analysis on the input than when his/her intentions are temporary.[52] A person's intention determines whether the storage of the information on the phenomenon is permanent or temporary. A different coding is used: a memory code for permanent storage and a perceptual role for temporary storage.

Different codes have different permanence. Codes of the sensory aspects of an input, such as appearance, are short lived. Hence, a person who looked at a word to decide whether it was printed in red or green would not remember the word's name very long because his coding would have emphasized color, not meaning. In contrast, a person who looked at a word to decide whether it was a synonym for some other word would form a semantic code, and he/she would remember the name of the examined word for quite a while.[53]

Stimulus and Attention and Recognition Processes

Upon observation of a triggering event or stimulus, the schema in the phenomenon is activated. The activation, as a process of detection, search, and attention, can be either a controlled or an automatic processing.[54]

Basically, automatic detection, triggered by the recognition of a stimulus, operates independently of the person's control. Automatic processing is the apprehension of stimuli by the use of previously learned routines that are in the long-term storage.

Automatic processing as learned in long-term store, is triggered by appropriate inputs, and then operates independently of the subject's control. An automatic sequence can contain components that control information flow, attract attention, or govern overt responses. Automatic sequences do not require attention, though they may attract it if training is appropriate, and they do not use up short-term capacity. They are learned following the earlier use of controlled processing that links the same nodes in sequence. In search, detection, and attention tasks, automatic detection develops when stimuli are consistently mapped to responses; then the targets develop the ability to attract attention and initiate responses automatically, immediately, and regardless of other inputs or memory load.[55]

In these automatic processes, no conscious effort is involved in the search as well as in demanding attention due to the learned sequence of the elements composing the schemata. On the other hand, controlled processes involve a temporary activation of novel sequences of processing steps that require attention, use short-term memory, and involve a conscious effort.

It is important to realize that in both processes, the use of schemata for encoding or retrieving information depends on accessibility in memory, where the accessibility of schemata is the probability that they can be activated, either for use in storage of incoming information or for retrieval of previously stored information.[56,57]

Accessibility of a schema depends upon such factors as the strength of the stored information, the extent of the overlap or match between input and schema, and the recency and frequency of previous activations. Each time a schema is activated for use, it becomes more accessible for successive activations. The instrumental effect of an activation on the accessibility of a schema is presumably a decreasing function of its prior strength. That is, a weak schema benefits more from an activation than a strong one.[58]

Empirical evidence on the increased accessibility of information with the frequency of activation is available.[59,60]

Retrieval Of Stored Information Needed For Judgment/Decision

Either the automatic or controlled search processes activate the appropriate schema for the phenomenon and allow the retrieval of information on the phenomenon. It is, however, the schema, a representation of the phenomenon, that is recalled rather than the actual phenomenon.[61-63] The effect becomes stronger as the time between observation and recall increases.[64]

The potential for different types of biases exists at this stage. For example, people may be more likely to recall information consistent with a schema confirming an expectation,[65] or may recall schema-consistent information which they never saw.[66] A good deal of evidence also suggests that schema-inconsistent information is more likely to be recalled[67] because of its novelty, saliency, and difficulty of incorporation into a schema.[68]

What is more likely to be recalled when faced with a phenomenon, what types of biases affect the recall of schemata of phenomena, and what can be done to reduce or eliminate the distortions in recall are some of the important questions in need of investigation. This model will assume that familiarity with the phenomenon through constant record keeping and other forms of monitoring may result in less biased recall. The solution, in fact, is more complex and depends on the type of relationship between memory and judgment. Reid Hastie and Bernadette Park investigated these relationships and distinguished between two types of judgment tasks, memory-based and on-line. They also identified five information-processing models that relate memory for evidence to judgment based on the evidence: (1) independent processing, (2) availability, (3) biased retrieval, (4) biased encoding, and (5) incongruity-biased encoding.[69]

With regard to the five information-processing models, the distinction is threefold: (1) cases where there is no relation between judgment and memory processes which include the independent processing model; (2) cases where memory availability causes judgment which include the availability-based information-processing model and the automatic search process described earlier; and (3) cases where judgment causes memory which include the biased retrieval, the biased encoding, and incongruity-biased encoding models. The biased retrieval model is selective in the sense that traces which "fit" the judgment are more likely to be found at the memory decision stage. Such biases have been termed *selective recall, confirmatory memory,* and *access-biased memory.*[70-73]

The biased encoding model assumes that biasing takes place at the time of the encoding of evidence information and memory search will locate a biased sample of information reflecting the initial encoding bias.

The incongruity-based encoding model assumes after the initial encoding, incoming information that is incongruent or contradictory is given special processing to enhance its memorability by being placed in "special tags" that strongly attach to memory. In memory search, the subject is more likely to find the incongruent information.[74,75]

This model assumes that where the phenomenon calls for an online task, the availability or automatic search model will characterize the retrieval of stored information needed for judgment decision. Selection of a processing model will depend on the individual objectives of the subject and the perceived consequences of his/her judgments on his/her economic and psychological welfare.

Reconsideration and Integration of Retrieved Information with OtherAvailable Information

At this stage the process involves the integration of the information retrieved from memory and other available information into a single evaluation of the phenomenon.

Where familiarity with the phenomenon is present and previously learned routines are retrieved active integration will not take place. An earlier integration is recalled from past stored output on the phenomenon. "What was once accomplished by slow, conscious, deductive reasoning is now arrived at by fast, unconscious perceptual processing."[76]

Where the phenomenon presents challenging and novel dimensions and where controlled processes were involved in attention and recognition, a cognitive integration of all the information is required to reach a single evaludation of the phenomenon. G. Mandler describes the process of "response learing" as follows:

First, the organism makes a series of discrete responses, often interrupted by incorrect ones. However, once errors are dropped out and the sequence of behavior becomes relatively stable as in running a maze, speaking a word, reproducing a visual pattern the various components of the total behavior required in the situation are "integrated." Integration refers to the face that previously discrete parts of a sequence come to behave functionally as a unit; the whole sequence is elicited as a unit and behaves as a single component response has in the past; any part of it elicits the whole sequence.[77]

Brunswick's lens model and Anderson's weighted average model provide support to the types of integration of information that take place.[78] The integration process is, however, also subject to various biases:

1. People may attach and give great weight to some type of information. For example, evidence in the employee appraisal literature shows that negative information has greater weight.[79,80]

2. There is evidence of an underutilization or underweighing of base rate or consensus information.[81]

3. There is ample evidence of the effect of various heuristics involved in decisions on and about a phenomena. They include (1) representativeness, (2) availability, (3) confirmation bias, (4) anchoring and adjustment, (5) conjunction fallacy, (6) hindsight bias, (7) illusory correlation and contingency judgments, (8) selective perception, (9) frequency, (10) concrete information, (11) data presentation, (12) inconsistency, (13) conservation, (14) nonlinear extrapolation, (15) law of small numbers, (16) habit/"rules of thumb," (17) "best-guess" strategy, (18) complexity in the decision environment, (19) social pressures in the decision environment, (20) consistency of information sources, (21) question

format, (22) scale effects, (23) wishful thinking, (24) outcome-irrelevant learning structures, (25) misperceptions of chance fluctuations (Gambler's fallacy), (26) success/failure attributions, and (27) logical fallacies in recall.[82]

The Judgment Process

The judgment process is the result of the integration process of information and the forming of a single evaluation of the phenomenon if the attention, recognition, and integration processes are the result of controlled processes. The judgment made in this case requires a conscious access to all the mental processes implied in the model. If, however, the attention, retrieval recognition, and integration processes were the result of automatic processes, the judgment is not and will not be conscious. It does not require the conscious use of all the mental processes implied in this model.[83,84] It is a routine judgment.

Routine judgment involves the rapid matching of immediate perceptions to a template which provides, and executes, a specific response, "if total debts do not equal total credits, re-add the total balance."

In the above example, there is no awareness of how the brain actually decides that the debits do not equal the credits. Even if awareness were possible, it is not normally necessary a great many of our routine activities, such as keeping our eyes open or holding our pencils, are done without any particular conscious awareness, at least until something causes us to become aware.[85]

Decision/Action (Response)

The final step of the model is the decision or selection of a response to the phenomenon. It is a conscious response preference resulting from the judgment process. It is an output of the judgment process and is clearly influenced by all the mental processes and biases described earlier. As a result, a new schema on the phenomenon will develop that will be part of the knowledge structure or the phenomenon stored in long-term memory.

The move from judgment to decision is a bridging process. It assumes that no obstacles stand in the way.

The decision/action has been investigated in various environments and using various phenomena. It has been found to differ from various normative decision models, including Bayesian-decision theory and expected value models.[86,87]

The bridging process, however, will be influenced by the cognitive steps described in this model as well as by other factors including the possible consequences of the decision on the phenomenon. Gibbins, for instances, cites the following factors:

Personal attitudes may play a direct role, much as determining priorities within the search process. For example, some public accountants may use financial return as their first selection criterion; others may use moral propriety as their first. Personal attitudes can also play an indirect role, limiting past actions and thus limiting the experiences on which judgment guides are built. The applications of such attitudes to the judgment process need not be conscious-particularly for deeply ingrained beliefs.[88]

Conclusions

The essence of cognitive relativism in is the presence of a cognitive process that is assumed to guide the judgment/ decision process. The model in this chapter shows that judgments and decisions made about a phenomenon are the products of a set of social cognitive operations that include the observation of information on the phenomena and the formation of schemata that are stored in memory and later retrieved to allow the formation of judgments and/or decisions when needed.

Notes

1. W. l. Felix, Jr., and W. R. Kinney, Jr., "Research in the Auditor's Opinion Formulation Process: State of the Art," *Accounting Review* (Apr. 1988): 245-71.

2. F.C. Bartlett, *Remembering* (London: Cambridge University Press, 1932).

3. Ibid., 201.

4. Ibid, 197-98.

5. D. E. Rumelhart, "Schemata and the Cognitive System," in R. S. Wyer, Jr., and T.K. Srull, eds., *Handbook of Social Cognition* (Hillsdale, N.J.: Erlbaum, 1984), 1:162.

6. Ibid.

7. Perry W. Thorndyke and B. Hayes-Roth, "The Use of Schemata in the Acquisition and Transfer of Knowledge," *Cognitive Psychology* 11 (1979): 83.

8. Jean Mandler, "Categorical and Schematic Organization in Memory," in R. C. Ruff, *Memory, Organization and Structure* (New York: Academic Press, 1979).

9. Robert S. Wyer, Jr., and S.E. Gordon, "The Cognitive Representation of Social Information," in R.S. Wyer, Jr., and T.K. Srull, eds., *Handbook of Social Cognition* (Hillsdale, N.J.: Erlbaum, 1984), 2:82.

10. L. Ross, M. R. Lepper, and M. Hubbard, "Perseverance in Self-Perception and Social Perception: Biased Attribution Processes in the Debriefing Paradigm," *Journal of Personality and Social Psychology* 32 (1975): 880-92.

11. C. A. Anderson, "Inoculation and Counter-Explanation: Debasing Techniques in the Perseverance of Social Theories," *Social Cognition* 1 (1982): 126-35.

12. W. G. Chase and H. A. Simon, "The Mind's Eye in Chess," in W. G. Chase, ed., *Visual Information Processing* (New York: Academic Press, 1982).

13. M. T. H. Chi and R. Koeske, "Network Representations of a Child's Dinosaur Knowledge," *Developmental Psychology* 19 (1983):29-35.

14. J. H. Larkin, et al., "Models of Competence in Solving Physics Problems," *Science* 200 (1980): 1335-42.

15. K. B. McKeithen, et al., "Knowledge Organization and Skill Differences in Computer Programmers, *Cognitive Psychology* 13 (1981): 307-25.

16. D. G. Bobrow and D. A. Norman, "Some Principles of Memory Schemata," in D. G. Bobrow and A. M. Collins, eds., *Representations and Understanding: Studies in Cognitive Science* (New York: Academic Press, 1975): 25-32.

17. D. E. Rumelhart, " Schemata and the Cognitive System," in R. S. Wyer, Jr., and T. K. Srull, *Handbook of Social Cognition* (Hillsdale, N. J.: Erlbaum, 1984), 1:170.

18. W. F. Brewer and G. V. Nalsamura, " The Nature and Functions of Schemas," in R. S. Wyer, Jr. and T. K. Srull, *Handbook of Social Cognition,* (Hillsdale, N.J.: Erlbaum, 1984), 1:141.

19. R. S. Woodswork and H. Schlosberg, *Experimental Psychology* (New York: Holt, 1954).

20. C. Graesser, S. E. Gordon, and J. D. Sawyer, "Memory for Typical and Atypical Actions in Script Activities: Test of a Script Pointer + Tag Hypothesis," *Journal of Verbal Learning and Behavior* 18 (1979):503-15.

21. S. E. Taylor, and J. Crocker, "Schematic Bases of Social Information Processing," in E. T. Higgins, C. P. Herman, and M. P. Zanna, eds., *Social Cognition: The Ontario Symposium,* vol. 1 (Hillsdale, N.J.: Erlbaum, 1981).

22. H.Markus, "Self-Schemata and Processing Information about the Self," *Journal of Personality and Social Psychology* 38 (1980):231-48.

23. H. Markus, and K. P. Sentis, "The Self in Social Information Processing," in J. Suls, ed., *Psychological Perspectives on the Self,* vol. 1 (Hillsdale, N.J.: Erlbaum, 1982).

24. J. A. Bargh, "Attention and Automaticity in the Processing of Self-Relevant Information," *Journal of Personality and Social Psychology* 43 (1982):425-36.

25. T. J. Ferguson, B. G. Rule, and D. Carlson, "Memory for Personally Relevant Information." *Journal of Personality and Social Psychology* 44 (1983):251-61.

26. H. Rankus, "Self-Schema DNA Processing Information about the Self," *Journal of Personality and Social Psychology* 35 (1977):63-78.

27. N. A. Kuiper, "Convergent Evidence for the Self as a Prototype," *Personality and Social Psychology Bulletin* 7 (1981); 438-43.

28. N. Canton and . Mischel, "Prototypes in Person Perception," in L. Berkowitz, ed., *Advances in*

Experimental Psychology, vol. 12 (New York: Academic Press, 1979).

29. S. T. Fiske and S. E. Taylor, *Social Cognition* (New York: Random House, 1984), 154.

30. R. P. Abelson, "The Psychological Status of the Script Concept," *American Psychologist* 36 (1981):715-25.

31. Fiske and Taylor, *Social Cognition,* 169.

32. R. S. Malpass, H. Lavingnern, and D. E. Weldon, "Verbal and Visual Training in Face Recognition," *Perception and Psychophysics* 14 (1973): 285-92.

33. P. W. Linville and E. E. Jones, "Polonized Appraisals of Outgroup Members," *Journal of Personality and Social Psychology* 42 (1982): 193-211.

34. S. E. Taylor, et al., "Categorical Bases of Person Memory and Stereotyping," *Journal of Personality and Social Psychology* 36 (1978): 778-93.

35. R. Hastie, "Memory for Behavioral Information That Confirms or Contradicts a Personality Impression," in R. Hastie, et al., eds., *Person Memory: The Cognitive Basis of Social Perception* (Hillsdale, N.J.: Erlbaum, 1981).

36. Similar models have been proposed for the performance appraisal process. See, e.g., A. S. De Nisi, T. P. Cafferty, and B. M. Meglino, "A Cognitive View of the Performance Appraisal Process: A Model and Research Proposition," *Organizational Behavior and Human Performance* 33 (1984): 360-96; J. M. Feldman, "Beyond Attribution Theory: Cognitive Processes in Performance Appraisal," *Journal of Applied Psychology* 66/2 (1981): 127-48.

37. H. H. Kelly, "Attributions in Social Interactions," in E. E. Jones et al., eds., *Attributions: Perceiving the Causes of Behavior* (Norristown, N. J.: General Learning Process, 1972).

38. B. Major, "Information Acquisition and Attribution Processes," *Journal of Personality and Social Psychology* 39 (1980): 1010-23.

39. De Nisi, Cafferty, and Meglino, " Performance Appraisal Decistion," 367-68.

40. Hl Tajfel, "Social Perception," in G. Lidzey and E. Aronson, eds., *Handbook of Social Psychology*, vol. 1 (Reading, Mass.: Addison-Wesley, 1969).

41. P. Slovic, B. Fischoff, and S. Lichtenstein, "Behavioral Decision Theory," *Annual Review of Psychology* 28 (1977): 119-39.

42. R. S. Wyer and T. K. Srull, "Category Accessibility: Some Theoretical and Empirical Issues Concerning the Processing of Social Stimulus Information," in E. Higgins, C. Herman, and M. Zarma, eds., *Social Cognition: The Ontario Symposium,* vol. 1 (Hillsdale, N.J.: Erlbaum, 1981).

43. M. Snyder and N. Cantor, "Treating Hypotheses about Other People: The Use of the Historical Knowledge," *Journal of Experimental Social Psychology* 15 (1979): 330-42.

44. M. Snyder, "Seek and Ye Shall Find: Testing Hypotheses about Other People," in M. Higgins, E. C. Herman, and M. Zarma, eds., *Social Cognition: The Ontario Symposium* (Hillsdale, N.J.: Erbaum, 1981), 1:33.

45. E. B. Ebbesen, "Cognitive Processes in Inferences about a Person's Personality," in M. Higgins, E. C.

Herman, and M. Zarma, eds., *Social Cognition: The Ontario Symposium* (Hillsdale, N.J.: Erbaum, 1981), 1:55.

46. R. E. Nisbett and L. Ross, *Human Inference: Strategies and Shortcomings of Social Judgment* (Englewood Cliffs, N.J.: Trent and Hall, 1980), 7.

47. Wyer and Srull, "Category Accessibility."

48. Feldman, "Beyond Attribution Theory." 129.

49. M. Snyder and S. W. Uranowity, "Reconstructing the Past: Some Cognitive Consequences of Person Perception," *Journal of Personality and Social Psychology* 37 (1979): 1660-72.

50. E.Tulving, "Episodic and Semantic Memory," in E. Tulving and W. Donaldson, eds., *Organization of Memory* (New York: Academic Press, 1972).

51. R. C. Atkinson and R. M. Shiffrin, "Human Memory: A Proposed System and Its Control Processes," in K. W. Spence and J. T. Spence, eds., *Advances in the Psychology of Learning and Motivation Research and Theory,* vol. 2 (New York: Academic Press, 1968).

52. R. I. Craig, and R. S. Lockart, "Levels of Processing: A Framework for Memory Research," *Journal of Verbal Learning and Verbal Behavior* 11 (1972): 671-84.

53. R. Lachman, J. L. Lachman, and Earl C. Butterfield, *Cognitive Psychology and Information Processing: An Introduction* (Hillsdale, N.J.: Erlbaum, 1979), 274.

54. Walter Schneider and Richard M. Shiffrin, "Controlled and Automatic Human Information Processing: I. Detection, Search, and Attention," *Psychological Review* (Jan. 1977): 1-53.

55. Ibid., 51.

56. E. Tulving and Z. Pearlstone, "Availability versus Accessibility of Information in Memory for Words," *Journal of Verbal Learning and Verbal Behavior* 5 (1966): 381-91.

57. B. Hayes-Roth, "Evolution of Cognitive Structures and Processes," *Psychological Review* 84 (1977): 260-78.

58. P. W. Thorndyke and B. Hayes-Roth, "The Use of Shemata in the Acquisition and Transfer of Knowledge," *Cognitive Psychology* 11 (1979): 86-87.

59. J. Perlmutter, P. Source, and J. L. Myers, "Retrieval Process in Recall," *Cognitive Psychology* 8 (1976): 32-63.

60. B. Hayes-Roth and F. Hayes-Roth, "Plasticity in Memorial Networks," *Journal of Verbal Learning and Verbal Behavior* (1979).

61. Ibid.

62. G. Greenwald, "Cognitive Learning, Cognitive Response to Pervasion(?), and Attitude Change," in A. Greenwald, T. Brock, and T. Ostron, eds., *Psychological Foundations of Attitudes* (New York: Academic Press, 1960).

63. R. Schanke and R. Abelson, *Scripts, Plans, Goals, and Understanding* (Hillsdale, N.J.: Erlbaum, 1977).

64. T. K. Srull and R. S. Wyer, "Category Accessibility and Social Perception: Some Implications for the Study of Person, Memory and Interpersonal Judgments," *Journal of Personality and Social Psychology* 38 (1980): 841-56.

65. K. P. Sentis and E. Burnstein, "Remembering Schema Consistent Information; Effects of Balance

Schema on Recognition Memory," *Journal of Personality and Social Psychology* 37 (1979): 2200-11.

66. C. E. Cohen, "Pearson Categories and Social Perception: Testing Some Boundaries of the Processing Effects of Prior Knowledge," *Journal of Personality and Social Psychology* 40 (1981): 441-52.

67. S. E. Taylor, et al., "The Generalizability of Salience Effects," *Journal of Personality and Social Psychology* 37 (1979): 357-68.

68. R. I. Craig and E. Tulving, "Depth of Processing and the Retention of Words in Episodic Memory," *Journal of Verbal Learning and Verbal Behavior* 11 (1972): 671-84.

69. R. Hastie and Bernadette Park, "The Relationship Between Memory and Judgment Depends on Whether the Judgment Task Is Memory-Based or On-Line," *Psychological Review* 93/3 (1986): 258-68.

70. E. J. Learner, A. Blank, and B. Chanowitz, "The Mindlessness of Ostensibly Thoughtful Action; The Role of Placebo Information in Interpersonal Interaction," *Journal of Personality and Social Psychology* 36 (1978): 635-42.

71. E. E. Learner, "False Models and Post-Data Model Construction," *Journal of the American Statistical Association* 69 (1974): 122-31.

72. E. E. Learner, "Explaining Your Results as Accent-Biased Memory," *Journal of the American Statistical Association* 70 (1975): 88-93.

73. M. Snyder and W. Uranowitz, "Reconstructing the Past: Some Cognitive Consequences of Person Perception," *Journal of Personality and Social Psychology* 36 (1978): 941-45.

74. C. Graesser and G. V. Nalsamura, "The Impact of Schema on Comprehension and Memory," *Psychology of Learning and Memory* 16 (1982): 60-102.

75. Graesser, Gordon, and Sawyer, "Memory for Typical and Atypical Actions in Scripted Activities," 319-32.

76. Chase and Simon, "Perception in Chess," 55-81.

77. G. Mandler, "From Association to Structure," *Psychological Review* 69 (1962): 415-27.

78. Ahmed Belkaoui, *Human Information Processing in Accounting* (Westport, Conn.: Quorum Books, 1989).

79. D. L. Hamilton and L. J. Huffman, "Generality of Impression Formation for Evaluative and Non-evaluative Judgments," *Journal of Personality and Social Psychology* 20 (1971): 200-207.

80. R. S. Wyer and H. L. Hinlete, "Information Factor Underlying Inferences about Hypothetical People," *Journal of Personality and Social Psychology* 34 (1976): 481-95.

81. Belkaoui, Human Information Processing in Accounting.

82. Ibid.

83. J. Jaynes, The Origin of Consciousness in the Breakdown of the Bicameral Mind (Toronto: University of Toronto Press, 1978).

84. R. E. Nisbett and T. D. Wilson, "Telling More Than We can Know: Verbal Reports on Mental Processes," *Psychological Review* (May 1977): 231-59.

85. Gibbins, "Propositions about the Psychology of Professional Judgment in Public Accounting," 113.

86. Belkaoui, Human Information Processing in Accounting.
87. R. M. Hogarth, Judgment and Choice: The Psychology of Decision (Chichester: Wiley, 1980).
88. Gibbins, "Propositions about the Psychology of Professional Judgment in Public Accounting," 114.

References

Abelson, R. P. "The Psychological Status of the Script Concept." *American Psychologist* 36 (1981): 715-25.

Adelson, B. "When Novices Surpass Experts: The Difficulty of a Task May Increase with Expertise." *Journal of Experimental Psychology: Learning, Memory and Cognition* 10 (1984): 483-95.

. "Problem Solving and the Development of Abstract Categories in Programming Languages." *Memory and Cognition* 9 (1981): 422-33.

Anderson, C. A. "Inoculation and Counter-Explanation: Debasing Techniques in the Perseverance of Social Theories." *Social Cognition* 1 (1982): 126-35.

Atkinson, R. C., and R. M. Shiffrin. "Human Memory: A Proposed System and Its Control Processes. In *Advances in the Psychology of Learning and Motivation Research and Theory,* edited by K.W. Spence and J. T. Spence, vol. 2. New York: Academic Press, 1968.

Bargh, J. A. "Attention and Automaticity in the Processing of Self-Relevant Information." *Journal of Personality and Social Psychology* 43 (1982): 425-36.

Bartlett, F. C. *Remembering.* London: Cambridge University Press, 1932.

Belkaoui, Ahmed. *Human Information Processing in Accounting.* Westport, Conn.: Quorum Books, 1989.

Bobrow, D. G., and D. A. Norman. "Some Principles of Memory Schemata." In *Representations and Understanding: Studies in Cognitive*

Science, edited by D. G. Bobrow and A. M. Collins. New York: Academic Press, 1975.

Brewer, W. F., and G. V. Nalsamura. "The Nature and Functions of Schemas." In R. S. Wyer, Jr., and T. K. Scrull, *Handbook of Social Cognition* (Hillsdale, N.J.: Erlbaum, 1984), 139-50.

Canton, N., and W. Mischel. "Prototypes in Person Perception." In *Advances in Experimental Psychology,* edited by L. Berkowitz, vol. 12. New York: Academic Press, 1979.

Chase, W. G., and H. A. Simon, "The Mind's Eye in Chess." In *Visual Information Processing,* edited by W. G. Chase. New York: Academic Press, 1983.

"Perception in Chess." *Cognitive Psychology* 4 (1973): 55-87.

Chi, M. T. H., and R. Koeske, "Network Representations of a Child's Dinosaur Knowledge." *Developmental Psychology* 19 (1983): 29-35.

Chiesi, H. L., G. J. Spilich, and J. F. Voss, "Acquisition of Domain-Related Information in Relation to High and Low Domain Knowledge." *Journal of Verbal Learning and Verbal Behavior* 18 (1979): 257-73.

Cohen, C. E. "Pearson Categories and Social Perception: Testing Some Boundaries of the Processing Effects of Prior Knowledge." *Journal of Personality and Social Psychology* 40 (1981): 441-52.

Craig, R. I., and R. S. Lochart, "Levels of Processing: A Framework for Memory Research," *Journal of Verbal Learning and Verbal Behavior* 11 (1972): 671-84.

Craig, R. I., and E. Tulving, "Depth of Processing and the Retention of Words in Episodic Memory." *Journal of Verbal Learning and Verbal Behavior* 11 (1972): 671-84.

De Nisi, A. S., T. P. Cafferty, and B. M. Meglino. "A Cognitive View of the Performance Appraisal Process: A Model and Research Proposition." *Organizational Behavior and Human Performance* 33 (1984): 360-96.

Ebbesen, E. B. "Cognitive Processes in Inferences about a Person's Personality." In M. Higgins, E. C. Herman, and M. Zarma, *Social Cognition: The Ontario Symposium* (Hillsdale, N.J.: Erlbaum, 1984), 52-59.

Emby, C. and M. Gibbins. "Good Judgment in Public Accounting: Quality and Justification." *Contemporary Accounting Research* (Spring 1988): 287-313.

Feldman, Jack M. "Beyond Attribution Theory: Cognitive Processes in Performance Appraisal." *Journal of Applied Psychology* 66/2 (1981): 127-48.

Felix, W. L., Jr., and W. R. Kinney, Jr. "Research in the Auditor's Opinion Formulation Process: State of the Art." *Accounting Review* (Apr. 1988): 245-71.

Ferguson, T. J., B. G. Rule, and D. Carlson. "Memory for Personally Relevant Information." *Journal of Personality and Social Psychology* 44 (1983): 251-61.

Fiske, S. T., and S. E. Taylor, *Social Cognition* (New York: Random House, 1984), 154.

Fredeirick, D. M., and R. Libby. "Expertise and Auditors' Judgments of Conjunctive Events." *Journal of Accounting Research* (Fall 1986), 220-90.

Graesser, A. C., S. E. Gordon, and J. D. Sawyer. "Memory for Typical and Atypical Actions in Scripted Activities: Test of a Script Pointer + Tag Hypothesis." *Journal of Verbal Learning and Behavior* 18 (1979): 319-32, 503-15.

Graesser, A. C., and G. V. Nalsamura. "The Impact of Schema on Comprehension and Memory." *Psychology of Learning and Memory* 16 (1982): 60-102.

Greenwald, A. G. "Cognitive Learning, Cognitive Response to Pervasion(?), and Attitude Change." In *Psychological Foundations of Attitudes,* edited by A. Greenwald, T. Brock, and T. Ostron. New York: Academic Press, 1960.

Halpern, A. R., and H. G. Bower. "Musical Expertise and Melodic Structure in Memory for Musical Notation." *American Journal of Psychology* 95 (1982): 31-50.

Hamilton, D. L., and L. J. Huffman. "Generality of Impression Formation for Evaluative and Non-evaluative Judgments." *Journal of Personality and Social Psychology* 20 (1971): 200-207.

Hastie, R. "Memory for Behavioral Information That Confirms or Contradicts a Personality Impression." In *Person Memory: The Cognitive Basis of Social Perception,* edited by R. Hastie, et al. Hillsdale, N.J.: Erlbaum, 1981.

Hastie, R., and Bernadette Park. "The Relationship Between Memory and Judgment Depends on Whether the Judgment Task Is Memory-Based or On-Line." *Psychological Review* 93/3 (1986): 258-68.

Hayes-Roth, B., and F. Hayes-Roth. "Plasticity in Memorial Networks." *Journal of Verbal Learning and Verbal Behavior* (1979).

Hogarth, R. M. Judgment and Choice: The Psychology of Decision. Chichester: Wiley, 1980.

Jaynes, J. The Origin of Consciousness in the Breakdown of the Bicameral Mind. Toronto: University of Toronto Press, 1978.

Kelly, H. H. "Attributions in Social Interactions." In *Attributions: Perceiving the Causes of Behavior,* edited by E. E. Jones. Norristown, N.J.: General Learning Process, 1972.

Kuiper, N. A. "Convergent Evidence for the Self as a Prototype." *Personality and Social Psychology Bulletin* 7 (1981): 438-43.

Lachman, R., J. L. Lachman, and Earl C. Butterfield. *Cognitive Psychology and Information Processing: An Introduction.* Hillsdale, N.J.: Erlbaum, 1979.

Larkin, J. H., et al. "Models of Competence in Solving Physics Problems." *Science* 200 (1980): 1335-42.

Learner, E. E. "Explaining Your Results as Accent-Biased Memory." *Journal of the American Statistical Association* 70 (1975): 88-93.

"False Models and Post-Data Model Construction." *Journal of the American Statistical Association* 69 (1974): 122-31.

Learner, E. J., A. Blank, and B. Chanowitz. "The Mindlessness of Ostensibly Thoughtful Action: The Role of Placebo Information in Interpersonal Interaction." *Journal of Personality and Social Psychology* 36 (1978): 635-42.

Linville, P. W., and E. E. Jones. "Polonized Appraisals of Outgroup Members." *Journal of Personality and Social Psychology* 42 (1982): 193-211.

McKeithen, K. B., et al. "Knowledge Organization and Skill Differences in Computer Programmers." *Cognitive Psycholgoy* 13 (1981): 307-25.

Major, B. "Information Acquisition and Attribution Processes." *Journal of Personality and Social Psychology* 39 (1980): 1010-23.

Malpass, R. S., H. Lavingnern, and D. E. Weldon. "Verbal and Visual Training in Face Recognition." *Perception and Psychophysics* 14 (1973): 285-92.

Mandler, G. "From Association to Structure." *Psychological Review* 69 (1962): 415-27.

Mandler, Jean. "Categorical and Schematic Organization in Memory." In *Memory, Organization and Structure,* edited by R. C. Ruff. New York: Academic Press, 1979.

Markus, H. "Self-Schemata and Processing Information about the Self." *Journal of Personality and Social Psychology* 38 (1980): 231-48.

Markus, H., and K. P. Sentis. "The Self in Social Information Processing." In *Psychological Perspectives on the Self,* edited by J. Suls. Vol. 1. Hillsdale, N.J.: Erlbaum, 1982.

Nisbett, R. E., and L. Ross. *Human Inference: Strategies and Shortcomings of Social Judgment.* Englewood Cliffs, N.J.: Trent and Hall, 1980.

Nisbett, R.E., and T. D. Wilson. "Telling More Than We Can Know: Verbal Reports on Mental Processes." *Psychological Review* (May 1977): 231-59.

Perlmutter, J., P. Source, and J. L. Myers. "Retrieval Process in Recall." *Cognitive Psychology* 8 (1976): 32-63.

Rankus, H. "Self-Schema DNA Processing Information about the Self." *Journal of Personality and Social Psychology* 35 (1977): 63-78.

Ross, L., M. R. Lepper, and M. Hubard. "Perseverance in Self-Perception and Social Perception: Biased Attribution Processes in the Debriefing Paradigm." *Journal of Personality and Social Psychology* 32 (1975): 880-92.

Rumelhart, D. E. "Schemata and the Cognitive System." In *Handbook of Social Cognition*, edited by R. S. Wyer, Jr., and T.K. Srull. Vol. 1. Hillsdale, N.J.: Erlbaum, 1984.

Schanke, R., and R. Abelson. *Scripts, Plans, Goals, and Understanding.* Hillsdale, N.J.: Erlbaum, 1977.

Schneider, Walter, and Richard M. Shriffrin. "Controlled and Automatic Human Information Processing: I. Detection, Search, and Attention." *Psychological Review* (Jan. 1977): 1-53.

Schneiderman, B. "Exploratory Experiments in Programmer Behavior." *International Journal of Computer and Information Sciences* 5 (1976): 123-43.

Sentis, K. P., and E. Burnstein. "Remembering Schema Consistent Information: Effects of Balance Schema on Recognition Memory." *Journal of Personality and Social Psychology* 37 (1979): 2200-11.

Slovic, P., B. Fischoff, and S. Lichtenstein. "Behavioral Decision Theory." *Annual Review of Psychology* 28 (1977): 119-39.

Snyder, N., and N. Cantor. "Treating Hypotheses about Other People: The Use of the Historical Knowledge." *Journal of Experimental Social Psychology* 15 (1979): 330-42.

Snyder, M., and S. W. Uranowity. "Reconstructing the Past: Some Cognitive Consequences of Person Perception." *Journal of Personality and Social Psychology* 37 (1979): 941-45, 1660-72.

Srull, T. K., and R. S. Wyer. "Category Accessibility and Social Perception: Some Implications for the Study of Person, Memory and Interpersonal Judgments." *Journal of Personality and Social Psychology,* 38 (1980): 841-56.

Tajfel, Hl. "Social Perception." In *Handbook of Social Psychology,* edited by G. Lidzey and E. Aronson. Vol. 1. Reading, Mass.: Addison-Wesley, 1969.

Taylor, S. E., and J. Crocker. "Schematic Bases of Social Information Processing." In *Social Cognition: The Ontario Symposium,* edited by E. t. Higgins, C. P. Herman, and M. P. Zanna. Vol. 1. Hillsdale, N.J.: Erlbaum, 1981.

Taylor, S. E., J. Aoker, S. T. Fiske, M. Springer, and J. Winkler. "The Generalizability of Salience Effects." *Journal of Personality and Social Psychology* 37 (1979): 357-68.

Taylor, S. E., S. T. Fiske, N. L. Etcoff, and A. J. Ruderman. "Categorical Bases of Person Memory and Stereotyping." *Journal of Personality and Social Psychology* 36 (1978): 778-93.

Thorndyke, P. W., and B. Hayes-Roth. "The Use of Schemata in the Acquisition and Transfer of Knowledge." *Cognitive Psychology* 11 (1979): 86-87.

Tulving, E. "Episodic and Semantic Memory." In *Organizatino of Memory*, editecd by E. Tulving and W. Donaldson. New York: Academic Press, 1972.

Tulving, E., and Z. Pearlstone. "Availability versus Accessibility of Information in Memory for Words." *Journal of Verbal Learning and Verbal Behavior* 5 (1966): 381-91.

Waller, W. S., and W. L. Felix, Jr. "The Auditor and Learning from Experience: Some conjectures." *Accounting, Organizations and Society* (June 1984): 383-406.

Weber, R. "Some Characteristics of the Free Recall of Computer Controls by EDP Auditors." *Journal of Accounting Research* (Spring 1980): 214-41.

Woodswork, R. S., and H. Schlosberg. *Experimental Psychology.* New York: Holt, 1954.

Wyer, R. S. Jr., and S. E. Gordon. "The Cognitive Representation of Social Information." In *Handbook of Social Cognition*, edited by R. S. Wyer, Jr., and T. K. Srull. Vol. 2 Hillsdale, N.J.: Erlbaum, 1984.

Wyer, R. S., and H. L. Hinlele. "Informational Factor Underlying Inferences about Hypothetical People." *Journal of Personality and Social Psychology* 34 (1976): 481-95.

Wyer, R. S. and T. K. Srull. "Category Accessibility: Some Theoretical and Empirical Issues Concerning the Processing of Social Stimulus Information." In *Social Cognition: The Ontario Symposium,* edited by E. Higgins, C. Herman, and M. Zanna. Vol. 1. Hillsdale, N.J.: Erlbaum, 1981.

Cultural Relativism

History of the Theories of Culture

By the middle of the eighteenth century, efforts were being made to develop scientific theories of cultural differences. Cultural differences were then attributed to the different degrees of intellectual and moral progress achieved by different peoples. Scholars such as Adam Smith,[1] Adam Ferguson,[2] Jean Turgot,[3] and Denis Diderot[4] held this view of the role of progress in defining cultural differences. The nineteenth century saw the emergence of the concept of *cultural evolution,* which posited that cultures move through various stages of development. Scholars such as Auguste Comte,[5] George Wilhelm Friedrich Hegel,[6] and Lewis Henry Morgan[7] held this view of progression of cultures from one state to another. Morgan's stages were savagery, barbarism, and civilization.[8] In the case of Comte they included theological, metaphysical, and positivistic modes of thought.[9] In all these schemes culture was viewed as evolving in conjunction with the evolution of human biological types and races, an idea started with social philosophers such as Thomas Malthus[10] and Herbert Spencer[11] and espoused by Charles Darwin.[12] The resulting movement, called Social Darwinism, postulates that cultural and biological progress results from the free play of competitive forces in the struggle of individual against individual, nation against nation, and race against race. Karl Marx also espoused the nineteenth-century evolution-and-progress paradigm of culture.[13] In his case the stages were primitive capitalism, slave society, feudalism, capitalism, and communism. The idea was also expressed by Friedrich Engels.[14]

The early twentieth century saw the emergence of various challenges to the evolutionism theory of culture. One challenge, introduced by Franz Boas,[15] is known as historical particularism. Boas viewed each culture as having a long and unique history that offers the best way to understand it. In addition, cultural relativism holds that there are no higher or lower forms of culture and that the stages proposed by the evolutionists merely reflect their ethnocentrism. Another challenge to evolutionism, known as diffusionism, holds that cultural differences and similarities are merely the result of people imitating and borrowing from other cultures. However, diffusionism fails to recognize that similarities between societies may be caused by the effects of similar environments.[16] British challenges to evolutionism were functionalism and structural functionalism. Functionalism advocates the descriptions of recurrent functions of customs and institutions rather than the origin of cultural differences and similarities.[17,18] All attempts to study the origin of cultural differences were viewed as speculative history. This new opposition, coupled with Freud's interpretation of cultures in psychological terms, shifted the emphasis to culture and personality theories, where cultural beliefs and practices were related to individual personality.[19,20]

More recently, dissatisfaction with anti-evolutionism has led to a return to some of the evolutionary theories of culture, a phenomenon spurred by Leslie White's linking of energy to the evolution of culture.[21] His basic law governing the evolution of culture is as follows: "Other factors remaining constant, culture evolves as the amount of energy harnessed per year is increased, or as the efficiency of the means of putting energy to work is increased."[22] This new evolutionism movement gave rise to the cultural ecology approach, advocated by Julian Steward, who identified the causes of cultural differences and similarities as the interaction of natural conditions with cultural factors.

With the popularity of dialectical materialism, which stresses the internal contradictions of sociocultural systems, and "dialectical" revolutions toward communism,[23] the new evolutionism led to the emergence of cultural materialism, which attributed cultural differences to the material constraints or conditions affecting the conduct of life in each society.

The French contribution to the debate, advanced by Claude Levi-Strauss, is know as structuralism.[24] It stresses the similarities among cultures as a product of the structure of the human brain and of the unconscious thought processes, a structure characterized by binary contrasts.

Finally, despite the overwhelming evidence that culture is encoded in the brain rather than the genes, the units of biological heredity, there are still some racial determinism theories being offered to explain cultural differences. With the realization that most intelligence tests are culture-bound, and with increasing evidence of environmental influences, these theories do not constitute a dominant paradigm.

Concepts of Culture

The concept of culture has been subjected to various interpretations. In fact, some anthropologists have stated that culture in the abstract can be explained only by reference to specific cultures.[25] Anthropologists approach vulture in at least three different ways: (1) the cultural universals approach, (2) the value systems approach, and (3) the systems approach.[26]

The cultural universals approach focuses on identifying certain universals common to all cultures, which does allow an examination of cultures in terms of how they contribute to these variables. An example of such a list is provided by G. P. Murdock.[27]

The value systems approach focuses on classifying cultures according to value systems. Instruments used to assess values among cultures include the Allport, Varnon, and Lindzey instrument,[28] Morris's "way of life" instrument,[29] Kluckhohn and Stradbeck's value theory,[30] Sarnoff's human value index,[31] and Rokeach's value survey.[32]

The systems approach focuses on the systems that make up a given culture. P. R. Harris and R. T. Moran identified eight subsystems in a culture: kinship, education, economy, politics, religion, association, health, and recreation.[33]

Some anthropologists view culture as information doubly coded once chemically in the rain as memory, and once externally as a language, behavior, material, or document, and as a cultural pool from which each individual, each dyad, each group draws its particular culture.[34]

In short, culture remains the basis of anthropological research. Anthropologists differ as to what the concept of culture means, although they generally agree that it is learned rather than logically transmitted, that it is shared by the members of a group, and that it is the foundation of the human way of life.[35] There is also a consensus on the issue of cultural utility in the sense that cultural practices have "functions" or reflect a society's "adaptations to its environment.

[C]ulture is man's primary mode of achieving reproductive success. Hence particular sociocultural systems are arrangements of patterned behavior, thought, and feeling that contribute to the survival and reproduction of particular social groups. Traits contributing to the maintenance of a system may be said to have a *positive function* with respect to that system. Viable systems may be regarded as consisting largely of positive-functioned traits, since the contrary assumption would lead us to expect the system's extinction.[36]

[C]ustoms which diminish the survival chances of a society are not likely to persist... Those customs of a society that enhance survival chances are *adaptive* and are likely to persist. Hence we assume that, if a society has survived to be described in the annals of anthropology, much if not most of its cultural repertoires is adaptive, or was at one time.[37]

That cultural customs can be explained in practical materialist terms is well explained by anthropologist Marvin Harris in his popular *Cows, Pigs, Wars and Witches: The Riddle of Cultrue.*[38]

Various concepts of culture exist in anthropology suggesting different themes for accounting research.[39]

1. Following Malinovski's functionalism,[40] culture may be viewed as an instrument serving biological and psychological needs.

2. Following Radcliffe-Brown's structural functionalism,[41] culture may be viewed as an adaptive regulatory mechanism that unites individuals with social structures.

3. Following Goodenough's ethnoscience,[42] culture may be viewed as a system of shared cognitions. The human mind thus generates culture by means of a finite number of rules.

4. Following Geetz's symbolic anthropology,[43] culture may be viewed as a system of shared symbols and meanings.

5. Following Levi-Strauss's structuralism,[44] culture may be viewed as a projection of the mind's universal unconscious infrastructure.

Cross-Cultural Research

Approaches for Studying Cultures

There are at least six possible approaches to cross-cultural research:[45]

1. Parochial research is the study of one country conducted by local researchers. These are single-culture studies or domestic studies that assume the phenomenon researched to be universal.
2. Ethnocentric research attempts to replicate the findings in one culture in a second culture. These are second-culture studies searching for similarities between cultures.
3. Polycentric research is the study of one phenomenon in several cultures. These are studies in many cultures searching for differences and denying the universality of the phenomenon.
4. Comparative research focuses on identifying the similarities and dissimilarities in cultures around the world. These are studies contrasting many cultures..
5. The geocentric approach focuses on phenomena that apply in more than one culture. They are international management studies searching for similarities.
6. The synergistic approach focuses on creating universality while maintaining a certain level of cultural specificity.

Each of these types of research will address a different set of questions and will be based on different set assumptions.

The Search for Universals in Cross-Cultural Research

The establishment of universally valid laws is a worthwhile if not essential goal. Walter J. Lonner identified four consistent bases from which to make comparisons across cultures within a universalistic framework: biological, social, ecological, and psychological.[46] Basically a finite number of culture types are formed because three bases biological, ecological, and social converge in various patterns. Then the various types are compared along the psychological base. That comparison identifies an obvious array of universals in human behavior which far outweigh substantive differences.

For that matter culture (in the plural) may be viewed as an opaque veneer covering an essential universality or "psychic and romantic unity" just as the methodological characteristics of the earth's variable mantle stretch over a molten mass of common core substance. Understanding and explaining why are the veneer of culture is metaphorically "thick" in some places and "thin" in others is therefore of major interest to cross-cultural researchers in psychology.[47]

Fons J. R. Van de Vijver and Ype H. Poortinga identify the following categories of universals along a dimension of "experimental rigor" or "strictness": (1) conceptual universals, (2) functionally equivalent (weak) universals, (3) metrically equivalent (strong) universals, and (4) scalar equivalent (strict) universals.[48] They are defined as follows:

In sum, conceptual universals refer to molar, theoretical concepts without any reference to measurement scales;

functionally equivalent universals are concepts for which empirical referents have been specified and that are measured in qualitatively the same way in each culture; metrically equivalent universals are concepts that have the same metric but not the same scale origin across cultures, and strictly equivalent universals have the same scale with the same origin in each culture.[49]

Those electing not to search for universals opt generally for the "traditional" cultural anthropology approach known under such names such as cultural relativism, contextualism, ideography, or configurationism. They are "relativists" in that they maintain that culture must be understood on no one else's terms but their own. To the relativists, some obvious generalizations and anthropological insights such as "the family is universal" are termed "fake universals" or "vague tautologies and forceless banalities."[50]

A comparison of both approaches would characterize the comparative approach as essentially nomothetic, focusing on universals, generalizations, and similarities cross-culturally, and the relativist approach as essentially content-oriented, with ideographic interests, focusing on the detailed delineation of each culture and the importance of a holistic picture for valid interpretation.[51]

Both approaches have limitations. "Relativism in its extreme form foreclosed the possibility of cross-cultural generalization, whereas comparativism courted the danger of ethnocentrism in viewing cultures."[52]

The use of cross-cultural research may benefit from the use of both the comparative and the relativist approach. The relativist approach is necessary in order to understand the meaning of phenomenon in that it relates it to the myriad variables surrounding it. The comparative approach can follow if matters of contextual understanding are carefully considered. This strategy may be feasible using the following three-step procedure suggested by John W. Berry:

1. Aspects of behaviors may be compared only where functional equivalence can be demonstrated. 2. (a) Existing descriptive categories and concepts can then be applied to these behavior systems in a tentative way (imposed etic); (b) these must then be modified to the extent that they become an adequate description from within that system (emic); (c) shared categories can then be used to build up new categories valid for both systems (derived etic) and can be expanded (if desired) until they constitute a universal. 3. Instruments and techniques can then be devised, based upon the derived etic or universal, and satisfying the requirement of conceptual equivalences.[53]

Etic versus Emic Approaches in Cross-Cultural Research

A research strategy is best characterized by the way it treats the relationship between what people say, think, and do as subjects and what they say, think, and do as objects of scientific inquiry. The researcher may view the thoughts and behavior of participants from either the perspective of the participants themselves, or the perspective of the observers. The terms *emic* and *etic* as introduced by K. L. Pike in *Language in Relation to a Unified Theory of the Structure of Human Behavior*[54] allow such a distinction. He suggests that the linguistic distinction between phonemics and phonetics can be used to delineate two different approaches to the study of cultural phenomena. Phonemics studies the sound in one particular language whole phonetics focuses on generalizing from phonemic studies in separate languages to a universal scheme relevant to all languages. Accordingly, the "emic" (from phonemics) differs from the "etic" (from phonetics) approach in cross-cultural research.

Berry typifies the emic-etic distinction as follows:[55]

Emic Approach	Etic Approach
Studies behavior from within the system	Studies behavior from outside the system
Examines one culture	Examines many cultures, comparing them
Structure discovered by the analyst	Structure created by the analyst
Criteria are relative to internal characteristics	Criteria are considered absolute or universal

The etic approach takes the perception of the observer as the important ingredient for the generation of scientifically productive theories about the causes of sociocultural differences and similarities. Basically it studies behavior from outside the system and examines phenomena from many cultures in order to extract the common elements across cultures.[56] It has been eloquently characterized as follows:

Rather than employ concepts that are necessarily real, meaningful, and appropriate from the native point of view, the observer is free to use alien categories and rules derived from the data language of science. Frequently, etic operations involve the measurement and juxtaposition of activities and events that native informants may find inappropriate or meaningless.[57]

What if amounts to is that the person adopting the etic approach, as an outside researcher, has his/her own categories by which the world is organized. Extreme advocates of the etic approach elevate the researcher as the best judge of the adequacy of the description or the analysis and dismiss the subject's opinion as potentially interesting but irrelevant.[58] Cross-cultural research has also warned against the use of a "pseudo-etic approach," or as Berry calls it, "an imposed etic approach,"[59] which assumes that an emic dimension is etic when in fact there is no evidence to support such an assertion. Harry C. Triandis and Marvin Gerardo[60] give the example of administering an intelligence text in another culture without using the construct-validating procedures outlined by S. H. Irvine and W. K. Carroll[61] as an example of pseudo-etic given that cultures differ in their concepts of intelligence. Basically, a pseudo-etic approach would translate and use instruments composed of items reflecting Western conditions in other cultures with little regard for the reliability, validity, or relevance of the new instrument in the new culture.

The emic approach takes the perception of the participants as the most important ingredient for the generation of scientifically productive theories about a sociocultural system. Basically, it studies behavior from within the cultural system centering on the native, that is, the insider's or the "informant's" view of reality, and is therefore based on data from only one culture. Extreme advocates of the emic approach elevate the subject as the best judge of the adequacy of the research and analysis, and consider the subject's acceptance of the results of the research as a necessary and sufficient validation.[62,63] For example, *philotimo* is an emic concept that applies only in Greece. It refers to the extent to which the individual conforms to the expectation of his/her in-group.[64,65] Emic research techniques generally subsumed under the term *ethnoscience* include ethnosemantics (also known as ethnographic semantics or ethnographic ethnoscience), formal analysis, and componential analysis.[66] J. P. Spradley has operationalized many of these techniques of ethnoscience in a series of books.[67-69]

The emic-etic distinction helps in differentiating the particular from the universal. In the controversy centering on the choices of etic versus emic approaches, a consensus seems to be emerging toward the sue of combined etic and emic measures in cross-cultural research. For example, P. J. Pelto indicates that there is an "embedded emicism" in most anthropological field work with a focus on native viewpoints, meanings, and interpretations.[70] It follows, however, that as a researcher starts moving inductively up the levels of analysis searching for universal categories, an etic approach emerges. The emic categories are added to the etic categories to allow for a testing of propositions about human behavior.[71] Another example of the combination of etic and emic measures is suggested by Triandis[72] as a two-step approach. The first step elicits the concepts under study in both cultures, while the second step includes those attributes common to (etic) as well as frequently used in one culture but not in any other (emic).

Cross-cultural research will also be best served if it includes more emic (subjectivist/idiographic/qualitative/insider) perspectives to be later generally translated into etic (objectivist/quantitative/nomothetic/outside) terms.

Design of Cross-Cultural Studies

In general, analysis of variance models is used to represent the design of many cross-cultural studies. A set of stimuli is administered to subjects from different cultural groups and can be represented by the following analysis of variance model:[73]

$$X_{sp(c)} = R + S_s + P_p PC_{pc} + C_c + SC_{sc} + SP_{sp'}$$
$$SPC_{spc'} E_{spc}$$

where

R is the overall mean

S_s ($s = 1, \ldots\ldots, n_s$) is the main effect for stimuli

$P_p PC_{pc}$ ($p = 1, \ldots\ldots, n_p$) is the confounded effect for the main effect persons and the person by culture interaction

C_c ($c = 1, \ldots\ldots, n_c$) is the main effect for culture

SC_{sc} is the interation between stimulus and culture

$SP_{sp'} SPC_{spc'} E_{spc}$ is the confounding of the stimulus by person interaction, the stimulus by person by culture interaction, and the error term (E)

When the design of cross-cultural studies is represented by analysis of variance models, the stimulus by culture interaction is interpreted as bias.[74] basically the effects of culture are perceived as an index of a valid cultural difference when the stimulus of culture interaction is small or insignificant.

Another approach may be used to determine whether the measurement refers to more universal or more specific aspects of behavior.

The concept of generalizability introduced by L. J. Cronbach et al.[75,76] is suggested by Van de Vijver and Poortinga.[77] Basically the generalizability theory dictates that estimation of the variance components be made first in order to compute coefficients of generalizability. Two coefficients of generalizability are deemed most important: (1) the coefficient estimating the stimulus by culture interaction ($\hat{p}2(R_{sc})$); and (2) the coefficient estimating the combined contribution of the main effect of culture and the stimulus by culture interaction ($\hat{p}2(R_{c+sc})$). They are estimated as follows:

$$\hat{p}2(\mu_S C) = \frac{\sigma^2(SC)}{\sigma^2(SC) + \sigma_2(SP, SPC, E)/n^1 p}$$

$$\hat{p}2(\mu^{C+SC}) = \frac{\sigma^2(C) + \sigma^2(SC)}{\sigma^2(C) + \sigma^2(SC) + \sigma^2(P, PC)/n^1 p + \sigma^2(SP, SPC, E)/n^1 p}$$

where $n^1 p$ = np for full sample estimates and $n^1 p = 1$. The suggested methodology is as follows:

1. Undertake a standard investigation of the significance of the F ratio to estimate the variance components.

2. If $\hat{p}2(R_{sc})$ differs substantially from zero, a meaningful quantitative comparison of scores is possible across cultures. The concept is either a conceptual universal or a functionally equivalent universal.

3. If $\hat{p}2(R_{sc})$ is equal to zero, then investigate $\hat{p}2(R_{c+sc})$. If it differs substantially from zero, then consistent cross-cultural differences exist and the concept is deemed to be a strong universal characterized by the same metric but a different origin across cultures.

4. If $\hat{p}2(R_{c+sc})$ is equal to zero or small, there is evidence for a strict universal, whereby the scales have the same metric with the same origin across all cultures.[78]

In conclusion, "when consistent cross-cultural differences are observed and the researcher is willing to attribute these to real cross-cultural differences, circumstantial evidence is needed to validate this choice and to rule out alternative hypotheses."[79]

Cultural Relativism

The Cultural Relativism Model

Edward T. Hall has stated that "culture is man's medium; there is not one aspect of human life that is not touched and altered by culture. This means personalities, how people express themselves (including show of emotions), the way they think, how they move, how problems are solved, how their cites are planned and laid out, how transportation systems function and are organized, as well as how economic and government systems are put together and function."[80] Culture in essence determines the judgment/decision process. The model, as illustrated in Exhibit 2.1, postulates that culture through its components, elements, and dimensions, dictates the organizational structures adopted, the micro-organizational behavior, and the cognitive functioning of individuals, in such a way as to ultimately affect their judgment/decision process when they are faced with a phenomenon.

Operationalization of Culture

This model avoids the two main problems that had beset earlier operationalization and use of culture: the equating of culture with nations and the ad hoc use of culture as a residual factor in explaining the variations that had not been explained by other factors.[81] Culture is viewed as collective mental programming.[82] that is, an ideological system forming the backdrop for human activity and providing people with a theory of reality.[83] This backdrop is composed of distinct elements and includes definite dimensions.

Exhibit 2.1

Cultural Relativism

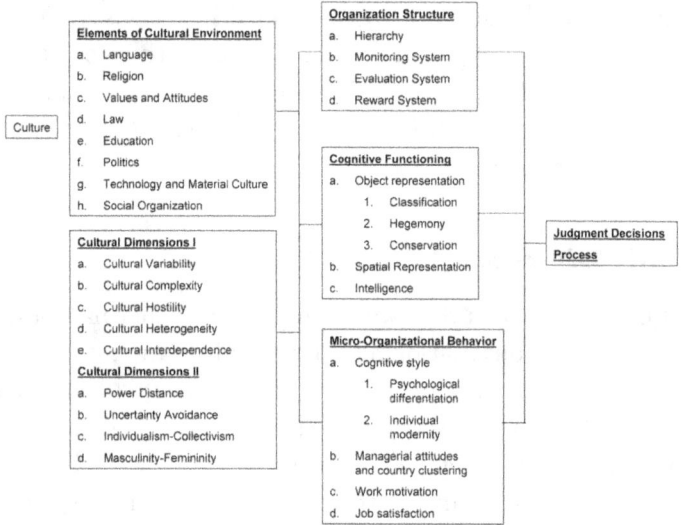

Those cultural elements generally assumed to affect the conduct of international business are language, religion, values and attitudes, law, education, politics, technology and material culture, and social organization. Each is assumed in this cultural relativism model to have the potential of dictating the organizational structures adopted, the cognitive functioning of individuals, and micro-organizational behavior, that may shape the judgment/decision process.

Cultures vary along five dimensions: cultural variability, cultural complexity, cultural hostility, cultural heterogeneity, and cultural interdependence.[84] The first three dimensions refer to conditions within cultures while the latter two refer to conditions among cultures. These dimensions may be seen as potential sources of problems for the multinational corporation:

(1) *Cultural variability* generates uncertainty, which calls for organizational flexibility and adaptability; (2) *Cultural complexity* raises the difficulty of understanding, which necessitates organizational and individual contexting and preparation; (3) *Cultural hostility* threatens goal attainment and survival which demands the maintenance of social acceptability; (4) *Cultural heterogeneity* hinders centralized decision making with information overload, which calls for decentralization; and (5) *Cultural independence* increases the vulnerability of an organization to intergroup conflict, which necessitates less autonomy for individual subsidiaries and move system-wide coordination.[85]

This cultural relativism model assumes that differences in these five dimensions generate different cultural environments that have the potential of dictating the organizational structures adopted, the cognitive functioning of individuals, and the micro-organizational behavior, that may shape the judgment/decision process.

Cultures also vary along four dimensions that reflect the cultural orientations of a country and explain 50 percent of the differences in value systems among countries:[86] (1) individualism versus collectivism, (2) large versus small power distance, (3) strong versus weak uncertainty avoidance, and (4) masculinity versus femininity.

Individualism versus collectivism is a dimension that represents the degree of integration a society maintains among its members or the relationship between an individual and his/her fellow individuals. While individualists are expected to take care of themselves and their immediate families only, collectivists are expected to remain emotionally integrated into in-groups which protect them in exchange for unquestioning loyalty.

Large versus small power distance represents the extent to which members of a society accept the unequal distribution of power in institutions and organizations. In large power distance societies, there is a tendency for people to accept a hierarchical order in which everybody has a place which needs no justification, whereas in small power distance societies, people tend to live for equality and demand justification for any existing power inequalities.

Strong versus weak uncertainty avoidance is a dimension that represents the degree to which the members of a society feel uncomfortable with uncertainty and ambiguity. In strong uncertainty avoidance societies, people are intolerant of ambiguity and try to control it at all costs, whereas in weak uncertainty avoidance societies, people are more tolerant of ambiguity and tend to live with it.

Masculinity versus femininity is a dimension that represents the nature of the social divisions of sex role. Masculine roles imply a preference for achievement, assertiveness, making money, sympathy for the strong, and the like. Feminine roles imply a preference for warm relationships, modesty, care for the weak, preservation of the environment, concern for the quality of life, and so on.

This cultural relativism model assumes that differences among these four dimensions create different cultural arenas that have the potential of dictating the organizational structures adopted, the type of cognitive functioning, and the micro-organizational behavior that may shape the judgment/decision process.

Culture and Organizational Structure

The cultural relativism model assumes that culture, through its elements and dimensions, dictates the type of organizational structure. The idea was first advanced by J. Child who stated that culture affects the design of organizational structure,[87] strongly refuting the "culture free" contingency theory of organizational structure proposed by D. J. Hickson and colleagues.[88-90] In fact, A. Sorge argued that all facts that bear upon organizational practices do so in the form of cultural constructs, and that organizations develop through a "nonrational" process of experimentation that is wholly cultured.[91]

There is no culture-free context of organization, because even if organizational solutions or contexts are similar, they are always culturally constructed and very imperfectly interpreted as the reaction to a given constraint. Culture enters organization through artful, unselfconscious, piecemeal experimentations with alternatives in business policy, finance, work/organization, industrial relations, education and training, and many other factors.[92]

Uma Sekaran and Carol R. Snodgrass carry the argument one step further by offering ideas on how specific cultural dimensions affect particular structural elements.[93] More specifically, they attempt to match the four structural aspects of the organization hierarchy, monitoring system, evaluation system, and reward system with the four cultural dimensions identified by Hofstede to synchronize with the preferred modes of behavior of organizational members.

Hierarchies refer to how organizations distribute power among their members while power distance refers to how a society accepts the fact that power in institutions and organizations is unequally distributed. It follows that the situation for large power distance culture groups calls for centralized and rigid hierarchies followed by emergent behavior of dependence and counterdependence while the situation for low power distance cultural groups calls for decentralized and fluid hierarchies followed by a behavior of independence.

The monitoring system refers to the process of collection and dissemination of information on performance, while uncertainty avoidance refers to the certainty of an unknown future and the difference in the way people react to it by experiencing different levels of anxiety. It follows that the situation for weak uncertainty avoidance calls for a simplistic monitoring system, while the situation for high uncertainty avoidance calls for a complete and comprehensive monitoring system followed by low levels of anxiety.

The evaluation system refers to the process of appraising the effectiveness and efficiency of organizational individual performance. Individual-collectivism refers to the type of relationship between a group and one of its members. It follows that a situation for individualistic cultural groups calls for an evaluation system based on individual achievement followed by a calculative behavior while a situation for collectivistic cultural groups calls for an evaluation system based on organizational performance followed by a moralistic behavior.

The reward system refers to the process of bestowing rewards for organizational or individual performance while masculinity-femininity refers to the nature of the social division of sex roles. It follows that a situation for "masculine" cultural groups calls for a reward system based on money, power, individual recognition and promotion, challenging assignments, status symbols, and the like, and catering to their machismo ideals, while a situation for "feminine" cultural groups calls for a reward system based on good quality of work life, security, a sense of belong, a cooperative work system, and catering to their androgynous ideals.

Micro-Organizational Behavior and Culture

Cross-cultural research on micro-organizational behavior has examined various issues including cognitive style, work motivation, job satisfaction, and other important managerial attitudes and behavior, and has highlighted the differences across various cultures.[94]

Research on cognitive style focuses on cultural differences in the structural aspects of an individual's cognitive system. It relied on the concept of psychological differentiation introduced by Witken, Dyk, Faterson, Goodenough, and Karp,[95] and used by Witkin and Berry,[96] for an understanding of the effects of subjective culture on individual behavior. Known as the theory of psychological differentiation it relies on field dependence and field independence measures to categorize people along the dimension of field of articulation. Cultural differences were found in the level of field articulation among cultural groups in several countries.[97] Besides the concept of field dependence, the cognitive style approach known as individual modernity was used in cross-cultural research to explain how cultures change from traditional to modern.[98]

Research on attitudes and values focuses on cultural differences rather than similarities in personal, work-related, and ancestral values and attitudes. Various studies focus on a clustering of countries in terms of managerial and worker attitudes and values. Simcha Ronen and Oded Shenkar present a review of the published literature on country clustering and propose a map that integrates and synthesizes the available data.[99] The variables examined in these clustering studies include work goal importance, need deficiency, fulfillment and job satisfaction, managerial and organizational variables, and work role and interpersonal orientation. The resulting clusters discriminate on the basis of language, religion, and geography. Well-defined clusters are the Anglo, Germanic, Nordic, Latin-European, and Latin American ones. Ill-defined clusters are those describing the Far East and Arab countries as well as countries described as independent (e.g., Israel and Japan). Areas in Africa haven not been studied at all while those in the Middle East and Far East have not been studied sufficiently. The review is, however, criticized by Peter Blunt[100] for alleged ethnocentrism and technocentrism defined as a lack of interdisciplinary approach in organizational studies.

Research on work motivation examines cross-cultural differences in motivation using one of the following theoretical bases: Atkinson's expectancy theory,[101] McClelland's achievement motivational theory,[102] vocation- and achievement-related motivation,[103] Adam's equity theory.[104]

Research on job satisfaction focuses on cross-cultural differences in the relationships between satisfaction and other variables of interest, such as absenteeism or productivity. These studies rely on the following theoretical bases: Maslow's need theory,[105] the importance of various job dimentions,[106] frame reference theory,[107] environmental theory,[108] Herzberg's two-factor theory,[109] and the alienation hypothesis.[110]

Cognitive Functioning

How people learn and think represents the study of human cognition. Cultural differences in cognitive functioning have also been subject to debate. Do people from different cultures perform differently on tasks that require certain cognitive skills? Two general hypotheses have been proposed. One maintains that cognitive processes are similar in individuals in different cultures, the other that cognitive processes are subject to cultural differences.[111,112] Evidence has been presented in support of both positions.[113,114] A third "situationist" hypothesis argues that cultural differences depend on the particular situation in the sense that "cultural differences in cognition reside more in the situation in the sense that "cultural differences in cognition reside more in the situations in which particular cognitive processes are applied than in the existence of a process in one cultural group and its absence in another."[115]

The debate needs to be continued to determine whether people from different culture will perform differently on tasks that require certain cognitive skills. Certain conditions need to be met in order to be able to usefully interpret potential cultural differences in cognitive functioning in a context.

When we consider intellectual growth or style in different cultures, we are confronted by three requirements. We need to obtain...some picture of skills common to people from many backgrounds, as well as skills that differentiate among them. At the same time, we need to find the features of milieu that may account for the similarities and differences in skills. And finally, ...we have to ask as we transpose a task from one culture to another, whether the same answer means the same thing in both worlds.[116]

To meet these requirements, two conditions need to be met. One is to assure the absence of ambiguous communication between the participants of the experiment and the preparers of the tasks, as differences in the way people perform may reflect different understandings of the requirements rather than differences in cognitive functioning. The second is to insure that the participants are truly representative of their respective cultures.

Are there any differences in the cognitive strategies used by people from different cultures when they represent information about objects? To answer this question, various studies have examined potential differences in classification, memory, and conservation.

There may be cultural differences in the way people classify objects, through the use of different attributes. Cultural differences in classification tasks have been observed although the variation may be attributable in some cases to differences in education and differences in familiarity with the items to be classified.[117] Similarly cultural differences in ability to abstract or to think in generalities have been observed in sorting tasks. However, in constrained classification tasks where the subjects learn to identify objects consistently on the basis of some feature, the skill in performing the task increases with age[118] and with education level.[119]

The recall of information from memory and its relation to culture is another research question of interest to object representation. In most experiments assessing the potential for cultural differences in the recall of information, age and education level were better related to the ways people from different cultures assess their memories.[120-122]

The concept of conservation, as introduced in Piaget's theory, refers to the ability of people to recognize the identity of objects or substances in spite of changes in their appearance. Cultural differences in the performance of conservation tasks are another research question of interest to object representation. While there are some obvious common problems due to differences in testing and scoring methods, age range of subjects, amount and kind of verbalization elicited from subjects, and language of testing, the results of experiments confirm the existence of a similar sequence of conservation across cultures and the existence of a "lag" in development of conservation among some cultures.[123-125] Education, although not necessarily formal, as well as familiarity with the task are also associated with differences in conservation performance.

Are there any differences in the cognitive strategies used by people from different cultures when they organize and use spatial information? Various studies have examined the potential for cultural difference in spatial reference systems. Different spatial reference systems were found to be used by Puluwat sailors navigating among the islands in the Western Pacific,[126] and the Temme in West Africa.[127] Other studies determined that cultural differences in the degree of filed dependence are a result of differences in child rearing and other socialization practices.[128] The evidence tends toward the existence of cultural differences in the organization and use of spatial information. More evidence is needed, however, to insure that the participants are more representative of their culture and are more familiar with tasks they can relate to.

There are also potential cultural differences in competence in cognitive behavior, which is equivalent to the Western notion of intelligence. A good definition follows:

Intelligence, a concept within the area of individual differences, reduces itself to two essentials, the power of the mind, and the skills through which this power expresses itself. The former aspect comes nearest to what the man in the street means by intelligence. It can be defined as "the ability to learn," "the capacity for understanding," "the ability to perceive essential relations between things," "insight into the nature of things." The "machines" through which this power expresses itself provide the foundation of abilities from the highest abilities such as the solving of mathematical equations, right down to the simplest such as trying one's bootlaces.[129]

Attempts to provide possible cultural bases for differences in general intelligence have been criticized for a number of reasons: (1) most tests of intelligence are culture-specific; (2) conceptual abilities are used as the skills to be assessed as intelligence while members of non-European cultures are known to think concretely;[130] (3) the environmental conditions between different cultural groups are not necessarily identical;[131] (4) contact with Western culture, familiarity with test materials, and conditions of testing affect the results;[132-134] (5) rural versus urban environment, education level, and early nutrition can also affect general intellectual development, a phenomenon known as the deficit hypothesis.[135] Berry, however, emphasizes that one must accept that it is clever to do different things in different cultural systems, and if inferences about intelligence are made, the original observations must be based upon an adequate sample of what people are able to do in their own cultural system.[136] A similar point is made by Vernon:

We must try to discard the idea that intelligence (i.e. intelligence b) is a kind of universal faculty, a trait which is the same (apart from variations in amount) in all cultural groups. Clearly, it develops differently in different physical and cultural environments. It should be regarded as a name for all the various cognitive skills which are developed in, and valued by, the group. In Western civilization it refers mainly to grasping relations and symbolic thinking, and this permeates to some extent all the abilities we show at school, at work, or in daily life. We naturally tend to evaluate the intelligence of other ethnic groups on the same criteria, though it would surely be more psychologically sound to recognize that such groups require, and stimulate, the growth of different mental as well as physical skills for coping with their particular environments, i.e., that they possess different intelligences.[137]

Conclusion

The essence of cultural relativism is the presence of a cultural process that is assumed to guide the judgment/decision process. The model in this chapter postulates that culture, through its components, elements, and dimensions, dictates the organizational structures adopted, micro-organizational behavior, and the cognitive functioning of individuals faced with a phenomenon.

NOTES

1. Adam Smith, *A Inquiry into the Nature and Causes of the Wealth of Nations* (London: J. Maynard, 1811).

2. Adam Ferguson, *An Eye on the History of Civil Society* (New York: Garland, 1971).

3. Anne Robert Jacques Turgot, *Reflections on the Formation and Distribution of Rides* (New York: A. M. Welly, 1963).

4. Denis Diderot, *Pensees FluConsophiques* (Geneve: E. Droz, 1950).

5. Auguste Comte, *A General View of Positivism* (London: Rutledge, 1907).

6. Georg Wilhelm Friedrich Hegel, *Lectures on the Philosophy of World History: Introduction* (New York: Cambridge University Press, 1975).

7. Lewis Henry Morgan, *Ancient Society* (New York: Holt, Rinehart and Winston, 1877).

8. Ibid.

9. Comte, *General View of Positivism.*

10. Thomas R. Nalthus, *An Essay on the Principle of Population* (London: T. Bensley, 1803).

11. Herbert Spencer, *Education: Intellectual, Moral and Physical* (New York: D. Appleton, 1961).

12. Charles Darwin, *The Descent of Man* (New York: H. M. Caldwell, 1874).

13. Karl Marx, *Capital* (Chicago: Encyclopedia Britannica, 1955).

14. Frederich Engels, *The Origin of the Family, Private Property and the State* (New York: International, 1979).

15. Franz Boas, *Anthropology and Modern Life* (New York: W. W. Norton, 1928).

16. R. J. Harner, "Population Pressure and Ten Social Evolutions of Agriculturalists," *South Western Journal of Anthropology* 26 (1970): 67-86.

17. Bronislaw Malinowski, *Argonauts of the Western Pacific* (New York: Dutton, 1950).

18. A. R. Radcliffe-Brown, *Structure and Function in Primitive Society* (London: Cohen and West, 1961).

19. Ruth Benedict, *Patterns of Culture* (New York: Houghton Mifflin, 1934).

20. Margaret Mead, *Coming of Age in Samoa: A Psychological Study of Primitive Youth for Western Civilization* (New York: Morrow, 1961).

21. Leslie White, *The Science of Culture* (New York: Grove Press, 1949).

22. Ibid., 368-69.

23. In the words of Karl Marx: "The mode of production in material life determines the general character of the social, political and spiritual processes of life. It is not the consciousness of men that determines their existence, but on the contrary, their social existence determines their consciousness" (*A Contribution to the Critique of Political Economy* [New York: International, 1970], 21).

24. Claude Levi-Strauss, *Le Cru and Le Cuit* (Paris: Pbon, 1964).

25. White, *Science of Culture.*

26. Simcha Ronen, *Comparative and Multinational Management* (New York: Wiley, 1986), 20-27.

27. G. P. Murdock, "Common Denominator of Cultures," in R. Linten, ed., *The Science of Man in*

the World Crises (New York: Columbia University Press, 1945), 12-42.

28. G. W. Allport, P. E. Vernon, and Q. Lindzey, *A Study of Values* (Boston: Houghton Mifflin, 1960).

29. C. Morris, *Varieties of Human Value* (Chicago: University of Chicago Press, 1956).

30. F. R. Kluckhohn and F. Strodtbeck, *Variations in Value Orientations* (Westport, Conn.: Greenwood Press, 1961).

31. I. Sarnoff, *Society with Tears* (Secaucus, N.J.: Citadel Press, 1966).

32. J. Rokeach, *The Nature of Human Values* (New York: Free Press, 1966).

33. P. R. Harris and R. T. Moran, *Managing Cultural Differences* (Houston: Cruff, 1979).

34. Paul Bohannan, "Rethinking Culture: A Project for Current Anthropologists," *Current Anthropology* 14/4 (Oct. 1973): 357-65.

35. Harris and Moran, *Managing Cultural Differences,* 8.

36. Marvin Harris, *Culture, Man and Nature* (New York: Thomas Y. Crowell, 1971), 141.

37. Carol R. Ember, and Melvin Ember, *Cultural Anthropology,* 3d ed. (Englewood Cliffs, N.J.: Prentice-Hall, 1981), 32.

38. Marvin Harris, *Cows, Rigs, Wars, and Witches: The Riddles of Culture* (New York: Vintage Books, 1974).

39. Linda Smircich, "Concepts of Culture and Organizational Analysis," *Administrative Science Quarterly* 28 (1983): 339-58.

40. B. Malinowski, *A Scientific Theory of Culture* (Chapel Hill: University of North Carolina Press, 1944).

41. A. R. Radcliffe-Brown, *Structure and Function in Primitive Society* (New York: Free Press, 1968).

42. Ward H. Goodenough, *Culture, Language and Society* (Reading, Mass.: Addison-Wesley, 1971).

43. Clifford Geertz, *The Interpretation of Cultures* (New York: Basic Books, 1973).

44. Claude Levi-Strauss, *Structural Anthropology* (Chicago: University of Chicago Press, 1983).

45. Nancy Adler, "A Typology of Management Studies Involving Culture," *Journal of International Business Studies* (Fall 1983): 24-47.

46. Walter J. Lonner, "The Search for Psychological Universals," in H. C. Triandis and W. W. Lambert, eds., *Handbook of Cross-Cultural Psychology* (Boston: Allyn and Bacon, 1980), 46.

47. Ibid., 147-48.

48. Fons J. R. Van de Vijver and Ype H. Poortinga, "Cross-Cultural Generalization and Universality," *Journal of Cross-Cultural Psychology* (Dec. 1982): 387-408.

49. Ibid., 351.

50. C. Geertz, "The Impact of the Concept of Culture on the Concept of Man," in J. R. Platt, ed., *New Views on the Nature of Man* (Chicago: Unversity of Chicago Press, 1965), 103.

51. R. L. Monroe and R. H. Monroe, "Perspectives Suggested by Anthropological Data," in H. C. Triandis and W. W. Lambert, eds., *Handbook of Cross-Cultural Psychology* (Boston: Allyn and Bacon, 1980), 254.

52. R. A. Lennie, *Culture, Behavior and Personality* (Chicago: Aldrine, 1973), 217.

53. John W. Berry, "On Cross-Cultural Comparability," *International Journal of Psychology* 4/2 (1969): 125.

54. K. L. Pike, *Language in Relation to a Unified Theory of the Structure of Human Behavior,* 2d ed. (The Hague: Mouton, 1967).

55. Berry, "On Cross-Cultural Comparability," 119-28.

56. J. W. Berry, "Introduction to Methodology," in H. C. Triandis and J. W. Berry, eds., *Handbook of Cross-Cultural Psychology,* vol. 2 (Boston: Allyn and Bacon, 1980).

57. Marvin Harris, *Cultural Materialism: The Struggle for a Science of Culture* (New York: Random House, 1979), 32.

58. Ibid.

59. Berry, "Our Cross-Cultural Comparability," 119-28.

60. Harry C. Triandis and Marvin Gerardo, "Etic Plus Emic versus Pseudoetic: A Test of a Basic Assumption of Contemporary Cross-Cultural Psychology," *Journal of Cross-Cultural Psychology* 14/4 (1979): 490.

61. S. H. Irvine and W. K. Carroll, "Testing and Assessment Across Cultures: Issues in Methodology and Theory," in H. C. Triandis and J. W. Berry, eds., *Handbook of Cross-Cultural Psychology,* vol. 2 (Boston: Allyn and Bacon, 1980).

62. C. O. Frake, "Cultural Ecology and Ethnography," in S. A. Dil, ed., *Language and Cultural Description: Essays by Charles O. Frake* (Stanford, Calif.: Stanford University Press, 1980), 18-25.

63. W. C. Sturtevant, "Studies in Ethnoscience," In A. K. Romney and R. G. D' Andrade, eds., *Transcultural*

Studies in Cognition (American Anthropologist Special Publication, 1964), 99-131.

64. H. C. Triandis and L. M. Triandis, "A Cross-Cultural Study of Social Distance," *Psychological Monographs* 76/21 (1962).

65. H. C. Triandis, E. E. Davis, and S. I. Takezawa, "Some Determinants of Social Distance among American, German and Japanese Students," *Journal of Personality and Social Psychology* 2 (1965): 540-41.

66. Nancy C. Morey and Fred Luthans, "An Emic Perspective and Ethnoscience Methods for Organizational Research," *Academy of Management Review* 9/1 (1984): 27-36.

67. J. P. Spradley, *The Ethnographic Interview* (New York: Holt, Rinehart and Winston, 1979).

68. J. P. Spradley, *Participant Observation* (New York: Holt, Rinehart and Winston, 1980).

69. J. P. Spradley, and D. W. McCurdy, *The Cultural Experience: Ethnography in Complex Society* (Chicago: Science Research Associates, 1978).

70. P. J. Pelto, *Anthropological Research: The Structures of Inquiring* (New York: Harper and Row, 1970).

71. Morey and Luthans, "An Emic Perspective and Ethnoscience Methods of Organizational Research," 30.

72. H. C. Triandis, *The Analysis of Subjective Culture* (New York: Wiley, 1972).

73. Van De Vijver and Poortinga, "Cross-Cultural Generalization and Universality," 405.

74. T. A. Cleary and T. L. Hilton, "An Investigation of Item Bias," *Educational and Psychological Measurement* 28 (1968): 61-75.

75. L. J. Cronbach et al., *The Dependability of Behavioral Measurements* (New York: Wiley, 1972).

76. L. J. Cronbach and P. E. Meehl, "Contrast Validity in Psychological Tests," *Psychological Bulletin* 52 (1955): 281-302.

77. Van de Vijver and Poortinga, "Cross-Cultural Generalization and Universality."

78. Ibid.

79. Ibid., 405.

80. E. T. Hall, *Beyond Culture* (Garden City: Anchor Books, 1977), 16-17.

81. J. Child, "Culture, Contingency and Capitalism in the Cross-National Study of Organizations," in L. L. Cummings and B. M. Staw, eds., *Research in Organizational Behavior* (Greenwich, Conn.: JAI Press, 1981), 3:303-56.

82. G. Hofstede, *Culture's Consequences: International Differences in Work-Related Values* (Beverly Hills, Calif.: Sage, 1980).

83. Uma Sekaran and Carol R. Snodgrass, "A Model for Examining Organizational Effectiveness Cross-Culturally," *Advances in International Comparative Management* (Greenwich, Conn.: JAI Press, 1986), 2:213.

84. Ven Terpstra, *The Cultural Environment of International Business* (Cincinnati: South Western, 1978), xvii.

85. Ibid., xxii.

86. G. Hofstede, "Dimensions of National Cultures in Fifty Countries and Three Regions," in J. B. Deregowski, S. Dziuarawiec, and R. S. Annis, eds.,

Explications in Cross-Cultural Psychology (Lisse, The Netherlands: Soviets and Zeilinger, 1983), 335-55.

87. Child, "Culture, Contingency and Capitalism in the Cross-National Study of Organizations," 313.

88. The argument that context-structure relations will be stable across societies is stated as follows:

89. This hypothesis implicitly rests on the theory that there are imperative, or causal relationships, from the resources of customers, of employees, of materials and finance, etc., and of operating technology of an organization, to its structure, which take effect whatever the surrounding societal differences. (pp. 63-64)

90. In D. J. Hickson, et al., "The Culture-Free Context of Organizational Structure: A Tri-National Comparison," *Sociology* 8 (1974).

91. D. J. Hickson, et al., "Grounds for Comparative Organizational Theory: Quicksands or Hard Core?" in C. J. Lammers and D. J. Hickson, eds., *Organizations Alike and Unlike* (London; Rutledge and Kegan Paul, 1979), chap. 2.

92. J. H. K. Inkson, D. J. Hickson, and D.S. Pugh, "Administrative Reduction of Variance in Organization and Behavior: A Comparative Study," in D. S. Pugh and R. L. Payne, eds., *Organizational Behavior in Its Context: The Aston Programme III* (Farnborough, Hants: Sasoon House, 1977), chap. 2.

93. A. Sorge, "Cultured Organization" (discussion paper 80-56, Berlin: International Institute of Management, 1980).

94. Ibid.

95. Sekaran and Snodgrass, "Model for Examining Organizational Effectiveness Cross-Culturally," 216-20.

96. Rabi S. Bhagat and Sara J. McQuaid, "Role of Subjective Culture in Organizations: A Review and Directions for Future Research," *Journal of Applied Psychology Monograph* (Oct. 1982): 653-85.

97. H. A. Witkin, et al., *Psychological Differentiation* (Potomac, Md.: Erlbaum, 1974).

98. H. A. Witkin and J. W. Berry, "Psychological Differentiation in a Cross-Cultural Perspective," *Journal of Cross-Cultural Psychology* 6 (1975): 4-87.

99. L. W. Gruenfeld, "Field Dependence and Field Independence as a Framework for the Study of Task and Social Orientations in Organizational Leadership," in D. Graves, ed., *Management Research: A Cross-Cultural Perspective* (Amsterdam, The Netherlands: Eisener North Holland Biomedical Press, 1973).

100. A. Inkeles and D. H. Smith, *Becoming Modern: Individual Change in Six Developing Countries* (Boston: Harvard University Press, 1974).

101. Simcha Ronen and Oded Shenkar, "Clustering Countries on Attitudinal Dimensions: A Review and Synthesis," *Academy of Management Review* 10/3 (1985): 435-54.

102. Peter Blunt, "Techno and Ethnocentrism in Organization Studies: Comment and Speculation Prompted by Ronen and Shenkar," *Academy of Management Review* 11/4 (1986): 857-59.

103. J. W. Atkinson, "Motivational Determinants of Risk Taking Behavior," *Psychological Review* 64 (1957): 359-72.

104. D. C. McClelland, *The Achieving Society* (Princeton, N.J.: Van Nostrand, 1961).

105. P. C. Smith, L. M. Kendal, and C. L. Hulin, *The measurement of Satisfaction in Work and Retirement: A Strategy for the Study of Attitudes* (Chicago: Rand McNally, 1965).

106. J. C. Adam, "Toward an Understanding of Inequity," *Journal of Abnormal and Social Psychology* 67 (1963): 422-36.

107. A. Maslow, *Motivation and Personality* (New York: Harper and Row, 1954).

108. F. Sahili, "Determinants of Achievement Motivation for Women in Developing Countries," *Journal of Vocational Behavior* 14 (1974): 297-305.

109. H. Soliman, "Motivation-Hygiene Theory of Job Satisfaction: An Empirical Investigation and an Attempt to Reconcile Both the One-and-Two Factor Theories of Job Attitudes," *Journal of Applied Psychology* 54 (1970): 452-61.

110. Ibid.

111. F. Herzberg, B. Mausner, and B. Snyderman, *The Motivation to Work* (New York: Wiley, 1959).

112. C. L. Hulin and M. R. Blood, "Job Enlargement, Individual Differences and Worker Responses," *Psychological Bulletin* 69 (1968): 41-55.

113. M. Cole, et al., *The Cultural Context of Learning and Thinking* (New York: Banc Books, 1971).

114. B. B. Lloyd, *Perception and Cognition: A Cross-Cultural Perspective* (Middlesex, England: Penguin, 1972).

115. H. C. Triandis, R. S. Malpass, and A. R. Davidson, "Psychology and Culture," *Annual Review of Psychology* 24 (1973): 356.

116. J. Kagan, M. M. Haith, and F. J. Morrison, "Memory and Meaning in Two Cultures," *Child Development* 44 (1973): 356.

117. M. Cole, J. Gray, J. Glick, and D. Sharp, *The Cultural Context of Learning and Thinking* (New York: Banc Books, 1971).

118. J. Goodnow, "Problems in Research on Culture and Thought," in D. Ekland and J. Flavell, eds., *Studies in Cognitive Developments* (New York: Oxford University Press, 1969).

119. P. M. Greenfield, "Comparing Dimensional Categorization in Natural and Artificial Contents: A Developmental Study among the Zimacantecos of Mexico," *Journal of Social Psychology* 93 (1974): 157-71.

120. A. C. Mundy-Castle, "An Experimental Study of Prediction among Ghancian Children," *Journal of Social Psychology* 73 (1967): 161-68.

121. M. Cole, J. Gray, and J. Glick, "Some Experimental Studies of Kjello Quantitative Behavior," *Psychonomic Monographs Supplements* 2 (1968): 173-90.

122. D. A. Wagner, "The Development of Short-Term and Incidental Memory: A Cross-Cultural Study," *Child Development* 45 (1974): 389-96.

123. S. Scribner, "Development Aspects of Categorized Recall in a West African Society," *Cognitive Psychology* 6 (1974): 475-94.

124. J. A. Meacham, "Patterns of Memory Abilities in Two Cultures," *Developmental Psychology* 11/1 (1975): 50-53.

125. P. R. Dasen, "Cross-Cultural Piagetian Research: A summary," *Journal of Cross-Cultural Psychology* 3 (1972): 23-39.

126. P. R. Dasen, "The Influence of Ecology, Culture and European Contact in Cognitive Development in Australian Aborigines," in J. Berry, and P. Dasen, eds., *Culture and Cognition: Readings in Cross-Cultural Psychology* (London: Methuen, 1974).

127. P. R. Dasen, "Concrete Operational Development in Three Cultures," *Journal of Cross-Cultural Psychology* 6/2 (1975): 156-72.

128. T. Gladwin, *East Is a Big Bird* (Cambridge, Mass.: Harvard University Press, 1970).

129. J. Littlejohn, "Cultural Relationism," *Anthropological Quarterly* 36, (1963): 1-17.

130. H. A. Witkin, et al., *Psychological Differentiation* (New York: Wiley, 1962).

131. S. Biesheuvel, "The Nature of Intelligence: Some Practical Implications of Its Measurement," in J. B. Jeffrey, ed., *Culture and Cognition: Readings in Cross-Cultural Psychology* (London: Methuen, 1974), 221.

132. A. G. J. Cryrs, "African Intelligence: A Critical Survey of Cross-Cultural Intelligence Research in African South of the Sahara," *Journal of Social Psychology* 57 (1962): 283-301.

133. S. Biesheuvel, "Psychological Tests and Their Applications to Non-European People," in J. B. Jeffrey, ed., *The Yearbook of Education* (London: Evans, 1949).

134. E. T. Abiola, "The Nature of Intelligence in Nigerian Children," *Teacher Education* 6 (1965): 37-58.

135. J. M .Faverge and J. C. Falmagne, "On the Interpretation in Intercultural Psychology: A Page Written in Recognition of the Work Done in This Field by Dr. S. Biesheuvel," *Psychologia Africana* 9 (1962): 22-36.

136. P. E. Vernon, "Administration of Group Intelligence Tests to East African Pupils," *British Journal of Educational Psychology* 37 (1967): pt. 3, pp. 251-82.

137. M. Cole and J. Bruna, "Cultural Differences and Influences about Psychological Processes," *American Psychologist* 26 (1971): 867-76.

138. J. W. Berry, "Radical Cultural Relativism and the Concept of Intelligence," in J. Berry and P. Dasen, eds., *Culture and Cognition: Readings in Cross-Cultural Psychology* (London: Methuen, 1974).

139. P. E. Vernon, *Intelligence and Cultural Environment* (London: Methuen, 1969), 10.

References

Abiola, E. T. "The Nature of Intelligence in Nigerian Children," *Teacher Education* 6 (1965): 37-58.

Acheson, J. "Accounting Concepts and Economic Opportunities in a Tarascon Village: Emic and Etic Views," *Human Organization* (Spring 1972): 83-91.

Adam, J. C. "Toward an Understanding of Inequity." *Journal of Abnormal and Social Psychology* 67 (1963): 422-36.

Adler, Nancy. "A Typology of Management Studies Involving Culture." *Journal of International Business Studies* (Fall 1983): 24-47.

Allport, G. W., P. E. Vernon, and Q. Lindzey. *A Study of Values.* Boston: Houghton Mifflin, 1960.

Atkinson, J. W. "Motivational Determinants of Risk Taking Behavior." *Psychological Review* 64 (1957): 359-720.

Belkaoui, A. "Cultural Determinism and Professional Self-Regulation in Accounting." *Research in Accounting Regulation.* Forthcoming.

————. "Managerial, Academic and Professional Influences and Disclosure Adequacy: For Empirical Investigation." *Advances in International Accounting.* Forthcoming.

————. "Is Disclosure Adequacy a Cultural or Technical Purpose?" Discussion paper, College of Business Administration, University of Illinois at Chicago, 1989.

————. *The New Environment in International Accounting.* Westport, Conn.: Greenwood Press, 1988.

————. *International Accounting.* Westport, Conn.: Greenwood Press, 1985, Chap. 2.

————. "Economic, Political and Civil Indicators and Reporting and Disclosure Adequacy: Empirical Investigations." *Journal of Accounting and Public Policy* (Fall 1983).

Belkaoui, A., A. Kahl, and J. Peyrard. "Informational Needs of Financial Analysts: An International Comparison." *International Journal of Accounting Education and Research* (Fall 1977): 19-27.

Benedict, Ruth. *Patterns of Culture.* New York: Houghton Mifflin, 1934.

Berry, J. W. "Introduction to Methodology." In *Handbook of Cross-Cultural Psychology,* edited by H. C. Triandis and J. W. Berry. Vol. 2. Boston: Allyn and Bacon, 1980.

————. "Radical Cultural Relativism and the Concept of Intelligence." In *Culture and Cognition: Readings in Cross-Cultural Psychology,* edited by J. Berry and P. Dasen. London: Methuen, 1974.

————. "On Cross-Cultural Comparability." *International Journal of Psychology* 4/2 (1969): 119-28.

Bhagat, Rabi S., and Sara J. McQuaid. "Role of Subjective Culture in Organizations: A Review and Directions for Future Research." *Journal of Applied Psychology Monograph* (Oct. 1982): 635-85.

Biesheuvel, S. "The Nature of Intelligence: Some Practical Implications of Its Measurements." In *Culture and Cognition: Readings in Cross-Cultural Psychology* (London: Methuen, 1974).

————. "Psychological Tests and Their Applications to Non-European People." In *The Yearbook of Education,* edited by J. B. Jeffrey. London: Evans, 1949.

Blunt, Peter. "Techno and Ethnocentrism in Organization Studies: Comment and Speculation Prompted by Ronen and Shenkar." *Academy of Management Review* 11/4 (1986): 857-59.

Boas, Franz. *Anthropology and Modern Life.* New York: W. W. Norton, 1928.

Bohannan, Paul. "Rethinking Culture: A Project for Current Anthropologists." *Current Anthropology* 14/4 (Oct. 1973): 357-65.

Child, J. "Culture, Contingency and Capitalism in the Cross-National Study of Organizations." In *Research in Organizational Behavior,* edited by L. L. Cummings and B. M. Staw, pp. 303-56. Vol. 3. Greenwich, Conn.: JAI Press, 1981.

Cleary, T. A., and T. L. Hilton. "An Investigation of Item Bias." *Educational and Psychological Measurement* 28 (1968): 61-75.

Cole, M., and J. Bruna. "Cultural Differences and Influences about Psychological Processes." *American Psychologist* 26 (1971): 867-76.

Cole, M., J. Gray, J. Glick, and D. Sharp. *The Cultural Context of Learning and Thinking.* New York: Banc Books, 1971.

————. "Some Experimental Studies of Kjello Quantitative Behavior." *Psychonomic Monographs Supplements* 2 (1968): 173-90.

Comte, Auguste. *A General View of Positivism.* London: Rutledge, 1907.

Cronbach, L. J., G. C. Gleser, H. Nanda, and N. Rajaratnam. *The Dependability of Behavioral Measurements.* New York: Wiley, 1972.

Cronbach, L. J., and P. E. Meehl. "Contrast Validity in Psychological Tests." *Psychological Bulletin* 52 (1955): 281-302.

Cryrs, A. G. J. "African Intelligence: A Critical Survey of Cross-Cultural Intelligence Research in Africa South of the Sahara." *Journal of Social Psychology* 57 (1962): 283-301.

Darwin, Charles. *The Descent of Man.* New York: H. M. Caldwell, 1874.

Dasen, P. R. "Concrete Operational Development in Three Cultures." *Journal of Cross-Cultural Psychology* 6/2 (1975): 156-72.

————. "The Influence of Ecology, Culture and European Contact in Cognitive Development in Australian Aborigines." In *Culture and Cognition: Readings in Cross-Cultural Psychology,* edited by J. Berry and P. Dasen. London: Methuen, 1974.

————. "Cross-Cultural Piagetian Research: A Summary." *Journal of Cross-Cultural Psychology* 3 (1972): 23-39.

Diderot, Denis. *Pensees FluConsophiques.* Geneve: E. Droz, 1950.

Ember, Carol R., and Melvin Ember. *Cultural Anthropology.* 3d ed. Englewood Cliffs, N.J.: Prentice-Hall, 1981.

Engels, Friedrich. *The Origin of the Family, Private Property and the State.* New York: International, 1979.

Faverge, J. M., and J. C. Falmagne. "On the Interpretation in Intercultural Psychology: A Page Written in Recognition of the Work Done in This Field by Dr. S. Biesheuvel." *Psychologia Africana* 9 (1962): 22-36.

Ferguson, Adam. *An Eye on the History of Civil Society.* New York: Garland, 1971.

Fons J. R., and Ype H. Poortinga. "Cross-Cultural Generalization and Universality." *Journal of Cross-Cultural Psychology* (Dec. 1982): 387-408.

Frake, C. O. "Cultural Ecology and Ethnography." In *Language and Cultural Description; Essays by Charles O. Frake,* edited by S. A. Dil, pp. 18-25. Stanford, Calif.: Stanford University Press, 1980.

Geertz, Clifford. *The Interpretation of Cultures.* New York: Basic Books, 1973.

———. "The Impact of the Concept of Culture on the Concept of Man." In *New Views on the Nature of Man,* edited by J. R. Platt, Chicago: University of Chicago Press, 1965.

Gladwin, T. *East Is a Big Bird.* Cambridge, Mass.: Harvard University Press, 1970.

Goodenough, Ward H. *Culture, Language and Society.* Reading, Mass.: Addison-Wesley, 1971.

Goodnow, J. "Problems in Research on Culture and Thought." In *Studies in Cognitive Developments,* edited by D. Ekland and J. Flavell. New York: Oxford University Press, 1969.

Goodrich, P. S. "Accounting and Political Systems." Discussion paper no. 109. School of Economic Studies, University of Leeds, 1982.

Greenfield, P. M. "Comparing Dimensional Categorization in Natural and Artificial Contents: A Developmental Study among the Zimacantecos of Mexico." *Journal of Social Psychology* 93 (1974): 157-71.

Gruenfeld, L. W. "Field Dependence and Field Independence as a Framework for the Study of Task and Social Orientations in Organizational Leadership." In *Management Research: A Cross-Cultural Perspective,* edited by D. Graves. Amsterdam, The Netherlands: Eisener North Holland Biomedical Press, 1973.

Hall, E. T. *Beyond Culture.* Garden City, N.Y.: Anchor Books, 1977.

Harner, R. J. "Population Pressure and Ten Social Evolutions of Agriculturalists." *South Western Journal of Anthropology* 26 (1970): 67-86.

Harris, Marvin. *Cultural Materialism: The Struggle for a Science of Culture.* New York: Random House, 1979.

————. *Cows, Rigs, Wars and Witches: The Riddles of Culture.* New York: Vintage Books, 1974.

————. *Culture, Man and Nature.* New York: Thomas Y. Crowell, 1971.

Harris, P. R., and R. T. Moran. *Managing Cultural Differences.* Houston: Cruff, 1979.

Hegel, Georg Wilhelm Friedrich. *Lectures on the Philosophy of World History: Introduction.* New York: Cambridge University Press, 1975.

Herzberg, F., B. Mausner, and B. Snyderman. *The Motivation to Work.* New York: Wiley, 1959.

Hickson, D. J., C. R. Hinings, C. J. McMillan, and J. P. Schmitter. "The Culture-Free Context of Organizational Structure: A Tri-National Comparison." *Sociology* 8 (1974): 59-80.

Hickson, D. J., C. J. McMillan, K. Azumi, and P. Horvath. "Grounds for Comparative Organizational Theory: Quicksands or Hard Core?" In *Organizations Alike and Unlike,* edited by C. J. Lammers and D. J. Hickson, chap. 2. London: Rutledge and Kegan Paul, 1979.

Hulin, C. L., and M. R. Blood. "Job Enlargement, Individual Differences and Worker Responses." *Psychological Bulletin* 69 (1968): 41-55.

Inkeles, A., and D. H. Smith. *Becoming Modern Individual Change in Six Developing Countries.* Boston: Harvard University Press, 1974.

Inkson, J. H. K., D. J. Hickson, and D. S. Pugh. "Administrative Reduction of Variance in Organization and Behavior: A Comparative Study." In *Organizational Behavior in Its Context: The Aston Programme*

III, edited by D. S. Pugh and R. L. Payne. Chap. 2. Farnborough, Hants: Sasoon House, 1977.

Irvine, S. H., and W. K. Carroll. "Testing and Assessment Across Cultures: Issues in Methodology and Theory." In *Handbook of Cross-Cultural Psychology,* edited by H. C. Triandis and J. W. Berry. Vol. 2. Boston: Allyn and Bacon, 1980.

Jaggi, B. L. "Impact of Cultural Environment on Financial Disclosure." *International Journal of Accounting Education and Research* (Spring 1982): 75-84.

Kagan, J., M. M. Haith, and F. J. Morrison. "Memory and Meaning in Two Cultures." *Child Development* 44 (1973): 356.

Kluckhohn, F. R., and F. Strodbeck. *Variations in Value Orientations.* Westport, Conn.: Greenwood Press, 1961.

Lennie, R. A. *Culture, Behavior and Personality.* Chicago: Aldrine, 1973.

Levi-Strauss, Claude. *Structural Anthropology.* Chicago: University of Chicago Press. 1983.

———. *Le Cru and Le Cuit.* Paris: Pbon, 1964.

Littlejohn, J. "Cultural Relativism." *Anthropological Quarterly* 36 (1963): 1-17.

Lloyd, B. B. *Perception and Cognition: A Cross-Cultural Perspective.* Middlesex, England: Penguin, 1972.

Lonner, Walter J. "The Search for Psychological Universals." In *Handbook of Cross-Cultural Psychology,* edited by H. C. Triandis and W. W. Lambert, pp. 46. 147-48. Boston: Allyn and Bacon, 1980.

McClelland, D. C. *The Achieving Society.* Princeton, N.J.: Van Nostrand, 1961.

Malinowski, Bronislaw. *Argonauts of the Western Pacific.* New York: Dutton, 1950.

―――. *A Scientific Theory of Culture.* Chapel Hill: University of North Carolina Press, 1944.

Marx, Karl. *A Contribution to the Critique of Political Economy.* New York: International, 1970.

―――. *Capital.* Chicago: Encyclopedia Britannica, 1955.

Meacham, J. A. "Patterns of Memory Abilities in Two Cultures." *Developmental Psychology* 11/1 (1975): 50-53.

Mead, Margaret. *Coming of Age in Samoa: A Psychological Study of Primitive Youth for Western Civilization.* New York: Morrow, 1961.

Monroe, R. L., and R. H. Monroe. "Perspectives Suggested by Anthropological Data." In *Handbook of Cross-Cultural Psychology,* edited by H. C. Triandis and W. W. Lambert. Boston: Allyn and Bacon, 1980.

Morey, Nancy C., and Fred Luthans. "An Emic Perspective and Ethoscience Methods for Organizational Research." *Academy of Management Review* 9/1 (1984): 27-36.

Morgan, Lewis Henry. *Ancient Society.* New York: Holt, Rinehart and Winston, 1877.

Morris, C. *Varieties of Human Value.* Chicago: University of Chicago Press, 1956.

Mundy-Castle, A. C. "An Experimental Study of Prediction among Ghancian Children." *Journal of Social Psychology* 73 (1967): 161-68.

Murdock, G. P. "Common Denominator of Cultures." In *The Science of Man in the World Crises,* edited by R. Linten, pp. 12-42. New York: Columbia University Press, 1945.

Nalthus, Thomas R. *An Essay on the Principle of Population.* London: T. Bensley, 1803.

Parsons, Talcott, and Edward A. Shils, eds. *Toward a General Theory of Action.* Cambridge, Mass.: Harvard University Press, 1950.

Pelto, P. J. *Anthropological Research: The Structures of Inquiring.* New York: Harper and Row, 1970.

Pike, K. L. *Language in Relation to a Unified Theory of the Structure of Human Behavior.* 2d ed. The Hague: Mouton, 1967.

Radcliffe-Brown, A. R. *Structure and Function in Primitive Society.* New York: Free Press, 1968.

―――. *Structure and Function in Primitive Society.* London: Cohen and West, 1961.

Rokeach, J. *The Nature of Human Values.* New York: Free Press, 1966.

Ronen, Simcha, and Oded Shenkar. "Clustering Countries on Attitudinal Dimensions: A Review and Synthesis." *Academy of Management Review* 10/3 (1985): 435-54.

Sahili, F. "Determinants of Achievement Motivation for Women in Developing Countries." *Journal of Vocational Behavior* 14 (1974): 297-305.

Sarnoff, I. *Society with Tears.* Secaucus, N.J.: Citadel Press, 1966.

Scribner, S. "Development Aspects of Categorized Recall in a West African Society." *Cognitive Psychology* 6 (1974): 475-94.

Sekaran, Uma, and Carol R. Snodgrass. "A Model for Examining Organizational Effectiveness Cross-Culturally." *Advances in International Comparative Management.* Vol. 2. Greenwich, Conn.: JAI Press, 1986, 213, 216-20.

Smircich, Linda. "Concepts of Culture and Organizational Analysis." *Administrative Science Quarterly* 28 (1983): 339-58.

Smith, Adam. *A Inquiry into the Nature and Causes of the Wealth of Nations.* London: J. Maynard, 1811.

Smith, P. C., L. M. Kendal, and C. L. Hulin. *The Measurement of Satisfaction in Work and Retirement: A Strategy for the Study of Attitudes.* Chicago: Rand McNally, 1965.

Soliman, H. "Motivation-Hygiene Theory of Job Satisfaction: An Empirical Investigation and an Attempt to Reconcile Both the One-and-Two Factor Theories of Job Attitudes." *Journal of Applied Psychology* 54 (1970): 452-61.

Sorge, A. "Cultured Organization." Discussion paper 80-56. Berlin, International Institute of Management, 1980.

Spencer, Herbert. *Education: Intellectual, Moral and Physical.* New York: D. Appleton, 1961.

Spradley, J. P., *Participant Observation.* New York: Holt, Rinehart and Winston, 1980.

————. *The Ethnographic Interview.* New York: Holt, Rinehart and Winston, 1979.

Spradley, J. P., and D. W. McCurdy. *The Cultural Experience: Ethnography in Complex Society.* Chicago: Science Research Associates, 1978.

Sturtevant, W. C. "Studies in Ethnoscience." In *Transcultural Studies in Cognition,* edited by A. K. Romney and R. G. D'Andrade, pp. 99-131. American Anthropologist Special Publication, 1964.

Terpstra, Ven. *The Cultural Environment of International Business.* Cincinnati: South Western, 1978.

Triandis, H. C. *The Analysis of Subjective Culture.* New York: Wiley, 1972.

Triandis, Harry C., and Marvin Gerardo. "Etic Plus Emic versus Pseudoetic: A Test of a Basic Assumption of Contemporary Cross-Cultural Psychology." *Journal of Cross-Cultural Psychology* 14/4 (1979): 490.

Triandis, H. C., and L. M. Triandis. "A Cross-Cultural Study of Social Distance." *Psychological Monographs* 76/21 (1962): 16-25.

Triandis, H. C., E. E. Davis, and S. I. Takezawa. "Some Determinants of Social Distance among American German and Japanese Students." *Journal of Personality and Social Psychology* 2 (1965): 540-41.

Triandis, H. C., R. S. Malpass, and A. R. Davidson. "Psychology and Culture." *Annual Review of Psychology* 24 (1973): 356.

Turgot, Anne Robert Jacques. *Reflections on the Formation and Distribution of Rides.* New York: A. M. Welly, 1963.

Van De Vijver, Fons J. R., and Ype H. Poortinga. "Cross-Cultural Generalization and Universality." *Journal of Cross-Cultural Psychology* (Dec. 1982): 405.

Vernon, P. E., *Intelligence and Cultural Environment.* London: Methuen, 1969.

―――. "Administration of Group Intelligence Tests to East African Pupils." *British Journal of Educational Psychology* 37 (1967): pt. 3, pp.251-82.

Violet, William J. "The Development of International Accounting Standards: An Anthropological Perspective." *International Journal of Accounting Education and Research* (Spring 1983): 1-13.

Wagner, D. A. "The Development of Short-Term and Incidental Memory: A Cross-Cultural Study." *Child Development* 45 (1974): 389-96.

White, Leslie. *The Science of Culture.* New York: Grove Press, 1949.

Witkin, H. A., and J. W. Berry. "Psychological Differentiation in a Cross-Cultural Perspective." *Journal of Cross-Cultural Psychology* 6 (1975): 4-87.

Witkin, H. A., R. B. Dyk, H. F. Faherson, D. R. Goodenough, and S. A. Karp. *Psychological Differentiation* Potomac, Md.: Erlbaum, 1974.

————. Et al. *Psychological Differentiation.* New York; Wiley, 1962.

Linguistic Relativism

Introduction

Speakers of different languages react differently to a phenomena, resulting in difficulties in interlinguistic communication internationally. Basically, the model in this chapter postulates that as a result of three theses: the linguistic relativity thesis, the sociolinguistic thesis, and the bilingual thesis, the linguistic characteristics dictate the judgment/decision process.

Linguistic Relativity in Accounting

The Sapir-Whorf Hypothesis of Linguistic Relativity

Anthropologists have always emphasized the study of language in their studies of culture. E. Sapir referred to the linguistic symbolism of a given culture. He perceived language as an instrument of thought and communication of thought. In other words, a given language predisposes its users to a distinct belief. All these premises led to the formulation of the principle of linguistic relativity: language is an active determinant of thought. Similarly, B. L. Whorf maintained that the ways of speaking are indicative of the metaphysics of a culture. Such a metaphysics consists of unstated premises which shape the perception and thought of those who participate in that culture and predisposes them to a given method of perception.[1]

Formulation of ideas is not an independent process, strictly rational in the old sense, but is part of a particular grammar, and differs, from slightly to greatly, between different grammars....We are thus introduced to a new principle of relativity, which holds that all observers are not led by the same physical evidence to the same picture of the universe, unless their linguistic backgrounds are similar, or in some way may be calibrated.[2]

The linguistic relatively hypothesis is in fact preceded by a linguistic determinism hypothesis. Linguistic determinism implies that the structure of language determines the structure of thought.

The deterministic aspect of such a position is well expressed by Whorf:

It was found that the background linguistic system (in other words, the grammar) of each language is not merely a reproducing instrument for voicing ideas but rather is itself the shaper of ideas, the program and guide for the individual's mental activity, for his analysis of impressions, for his synthesis of his mental stock and trade.

Formulation of ideas is not an independent process, strictly rational in the old sense, but is part of a particular grammar, and differs, from slightly to greatly, between different grammars. We dissect nature along lines laid down by our native languages. The categories and types that we isolate in the world of phenomena we do not find these because they stare every observer in the face; on the contrary, the world is presented in a kaleidoscopic flux by our minds and this means largely by the linguistic system in our minds.[3]

These arguments were used to demonstrate the relativity of language. Whorf went even further by showing that in certain domains American Indian languages are superior to European languages:

It takes but little real scientific study of preliterate languages, especially those of America, to show how much more precise and finely elaborated is the system of relationship in many such tongues than ours. By comparison with many American languages, the formal systematic organization of ideas in English, German, French, or Italian is poor and jejeune. Why for instance, do we not like the Hopi, use a different way of expressing the relation of channel of sensation (seeing) to result in consciousness, as between "I see that it is red" and "I see that it is new."? We fuse the two different types of relationship into a vague sort of connection expressed by "that" whereas the Hopi indicates that in the first case seeing presents unspecified evidence from which is drawn the inference of newness....Does the Hopi language show here a higher plane of thinking, a more rational analysis of situations, than our English? Of course, it does. In this field an din others, English compared to Hopi is like a bludgeon compared to a rapier.[4]

The basic view in the Sapir-Whorf hypothesis is that the characteristics of language have determining influences on cognitive processes. Basically monolingual individuals speaking completely different languages in terms of structural, grammatical, and other characteristics, should adopt different mediated behaviors.

The (real world) is to a large extent unconsciously built up on the language habits of the group. The worlds in which different societies live are *distinct* worlds, merely the same world with different labels attached. We [as individuals] see and hear and otherwise experience very largely as we do because the language habits of our community predispose certain choices of interpretation.[5]

Thus, language is more than a communication vehicle about objective reality existing independently of language but instead represents an objective reality that man uses to organize the realities around him. The scheme used by speakers of different languages when speaking about the nonlinguistic world will differ drastically. As stated by Sapir, "language does not as a matter of actual behavior stand apart from or run parallel to direct experience but completely penetrates with it."[6] Or as stated by Whorf, "observers are not led by the same picture of the universe, unless their linguistic backgrounds are similar or can in some way be calibrated."[7]

That the real world is to a large extent unconsciously built on the language of a given group and that the intellectual system embodied in each language shapes the thought of its speakers in a quite general way is the essence of the linguistic relativity hypothesis.

The categories and types we isolate from the world of phenomena we do not find these because they stare every observer in the face. On the contrary the world is presented in a kaleidoscopic flux of impressions which have to be organized in our minds. This means largely, by the linguistic system in our minds.[8]

In its extreme position, the linguistic relativity hypothesis claims that cognitive organization is directly constrained by linguistic structure. J. A. Fishman explains this claim as follows:

Some languages recognize far more tenses than do others. Some languages recognize a gender of norms (and, therefore, also required markers of gender in the verb and adjective systems), whereas others do not. Some languages build into the verb system recognition of certainty or uncertainty of past, present, or future action. Other languages build into the verb system a recognition of the size, shape and color of norms referred to.[9]

In a summary of the linguistic relativity hypothesis, Roger Brown distinguishes two main hypotheses:[10]

1. Structural differences between language systems will, in general, be paralleled by nonlinguistic cognitive differences, of an unspecified sort, in the native speakers of two languages.
2. The structure of anyone's native language strongly influences or fully determines the world-view he will acquire as he learns the language.[11]

Paul Kay and Willett Kempton add a third hypothesis:

1. The semantic systems of different languages vary without constraint.[12]

The evidence on the three hypotheses is, however, mixed.

That the linguistic relatively hypothesis indicates that the characteristics of language have determining influences on cognitive processes generates both delight and horror. The delight resides in the knowledge that the mastery of the language is followed by the influence on our cognitive abilities. Fishman, however, mentions the horror:

The first is the *horror of helplessness,* since all of us in most walks of life and most of us in all walks of life are helplessly trapped by the language we speak. We cannot escape from it and, even if we could flee, where would we turn but to some other language with its own blinders and its own vic-elike embrace on what we think, what we perceive, and what we say. The second horror is the *horror of hopelessness* for what hope can there be for mankind? What hope that our group will ever understand the other? What hope that one nation will ever communicate with the other?[13]

While these two horrors are exaggerated, the challenge remains to understand the full consequences of the linguistic relativity thesis in the social sciences in general.

Systematization of the Sapir-Whorf Hypothesis

Using a double dichotomy, Fishman systematized the Sapir-Whorf hypothesis as shown in Exhibit 3.1.[14] Fishman's model views the characteristics of language as either lexical or grammatical, and the behavior of the speaker as either verbal behavior per se (generally interpreted in terms of cultural themes or *Weltanschauung*) and individual behavior data which is nonverbal in nature. Four cells correspond to four levels of the Sapir-Whorf hypothesis of linguistic relativity.

Exhibit 3.1

Fishman's Systematic Version of the Sapir-Whorf Hypothesis

Data about language characteristics	Data of Speaker's Behavior	
	Linguistic Data	Nonlinguistic Data
Lexical Characteristic	1	2
Grammatical Characteristics	3	4

Cell I corresponds to linguistic codifiability and cultural reflections. It implies a relationship between the lexical properties of a language and the speaker's linguistic behavior. Phenomena are codified differently in each language, which structures their verbal behavior. The absence of an English equivalent for German *Gemutlichkeit* makes it easier for Germans to be aware of and to express the phenomena. The French use of one word for both "conscience" and "consciousness" is shown by R. Linderman to have led to a greater conceptual fusion between these two usages on the part of French philosophers than for English or German thinkers.[15] Because of the different codifications the linguistic behavior and communication will differ. For example, the fact that Arabs have different terms for horses and the Eskimos have different terms for snow, makes it easier for Arabs to communicate about horses and Eskimos about snow. This analysis is applicable to R. D. Gastil's concept of polysemy that may be more easily expressible in one language than another.[16]

Languages differ as to the presence or absence of the field distinctions which they make. A language may be seen as a limited group of words and forms available for the sue of a man thinking or expressing himself in the medium of that language. If he does not have the means to do a certain job of thinking or expressing, that job will not be accomplished as well as if he had such means.[17]

Cell 2 corresponds to linguistic codifiability and behavioral concomitants. It implies a relationship between lexical properties of a language and then on linguistic behavior of the users of a lanauge. This level is more crucial than level I for the testing of the linguistic relativity hypothesis.

In order to find evidence to support the linguistic relatively hypothesis it is not sufficient merely to point to differences between languages and to assume that users of these languages have correspondingly different mental experiences. If we are not to be guilty of circular inference, it is necessary to show some correspondence between the presence or absence of a certain linguistic phenomenon and the presence or absence of a certain kind of non-linguistic response.[18]

The second level implies that speakers of a language that make certain lexical distinctions will be able to perform certain nonlinguistic tasks better and more rapidly than the speakers of language that do make these lexical distinctions. R. W. Brown and E. H. Lenneberg,[19] Lenneberg,[20,21] and De Lee Lantz and Volney Steffbre[22] showed a shorter response latency in naming culturally encoded colors (i.e., colors that can be named with a single word) than colors which are not culturally encoded.

Cell 3 corresponds to linguistic structure and its cultural concomitants. It implies a relationship between grammatical characteristics and linguistic behavior. In essence, the concern is with the relation between language and worldview. It is best illustrated by Whorf's statement:

The background linguistic system (in other words, the grammar) of each language is not merely a reproducing instrument for voicing ideas, but rather is itself the shaper of ideas, the program and guide for the individual's mental activity, for his analysis of impressions, for his synthesis of his mental stock in trade. Formulation of ideas is not an independent process, strictly rational in the old sense, but is part of a particular grammar and differs, from slightly to greatly, between grammars.[23]

The thesis is best echoed by G. L. Trager:

Language as whole has structure and all its parts and subdivisions also have structure....[If] the rest of cultural behavior has been conditioned by language, then there must be a relationship between *the structure* of language and the *structure* of behavior.[24]

Basically the level of the hypothesis in cell 3 assumes that speakers of one language who use specific grammatical rules are predisposed to a given worldview different from the speakers of other languages. Whorf bases his conclusions on an analysis of Hopi and compares it with standard average European languages (SAE) (including English).[25] He highlights specific grammatical structures (absence of tenses, the classification of events by duration categories, the use of grammatical forms to indicate the type of validity intended by the speaker, etc.). H. Hoijer argued the same position by analyzing Navaho.[26] The work of Susan

Ervin-Tripp on bilingualism may also be used to support this level of the linguistic relativity hypothesis.[27] Bilingual Japanese women married to U.S. servicemen were asked to converse in Japanese with the result that the context of their conversation was more typical of women in Japan. When asked to converse in English, the context was more typical of women I the United States.

Cell 4 corresponds to the linguistic structure and its behavioral concomitants. It implies a relationship between grammatical characteristics and nonlinguistic behavior. J. B. Carroll and T. S. Casagrande provide support for this level of the hypothesis.[28] They examined whether the speakers of language that codes verbally for color, shape, and size, as the Navaho language, will classify objects differently from the speakers of a language that codes verbally for tense, person, and number, as in English.

(a) ... This feature of the Navaho language would affect the relative potency or order of emergency of such concepts as colour, size, shape or form, and number in the Navaho-speaking child (specifically that shape or form would develop earlier and increase more regularly with age, since this is the aspect provided for in the verb forms themselves), and (b) that he (i.e. the Navaho child) would be more inclined to perceive formal similarities (i.e. shape or form similarities) between objects than would English-speaking Navaho children of the same age.[29]

The result showed that Navaho-dominant Navahos made object choice as predicted by the grammatical verb more often than did the English-dominant Navahos.

The Sociolinguistic Thesis

Speech systems are generated, or controlled, by social relations. This role of language in defining communities and social relationships is the realm of sociolinguistics. It argues that the roots of social class are carried through a communication code that social class itself promotes.

If a social group, by virtue of its class relation, i.e., as a result of its common occupational function and social status, has developed strong communal bonds; if the work relations of this group offer little variety; little exercise in decision making; if asserting, if it is to be successful must be a collective rather than an individual act; if the work task requires physical manipulation and control rather than symbolic organization and control; if the diminished authority of the man at work is transformed into an authority of power at home; if the home is over crowded and limits the variety of situations it can offer; if the children socialize each other in an environment offering little intellectual stimuli; if all these attributes are found in one setting, then it is plausible to assume that such a social setting will generate a particular form of communication which will shape the intellectual, social and affective orientation of the children.[30]

The linguistic thesis implies that different forms of social relations generate very different speech systems, linguistic repertoires, or communications codes.[31-34] In other words, people learn their social roles through the process of communication. Social role is best defined as follows: "A social role can then be considered as a complex coding activity controlling both the creation and organization of specific meaning and the conditions for their transmission and reception.[35]

Communication codes can be either elaborated or restricted, depending whether it is difficult or easy to predict their linguistic alternatives. Similarly role systems are either open or closed, according to whether they permit or reduce the range of alternatives for realization of verbal meanings. Basil Bernstein used this simple dichotomy to identify the contextual nature of the use of repertories and to show a causal connection between role systems, communication codes, and the realization of different orders of meaning and relevance. As shown in Exhibit 3.2, in distinguishing between object and person orders of meaning, an individual will use an elaborated or restricted code depending on whether the role system is closed and the verbal meanings are likely to be assigned or the role system is open and the verbal meanings are likely to be novel. As stated by Bernstein:

We can begin to see that in the area where the role system is open, there is an induced motivation to explore and actively seek out and extend meanings; where the role is closed, there is little induced motivation to explore and create novel meanings....

Where the role system is open, the individual child learns to cope with ambiguity and isolation in the creation of verbal meaning; where the role system is closed, the individual or child forges such learning. On the contrary, he learns to create verbal meanings in social contexts which are unambiguous and communalized.[36]

Thus the social role determines the communication code or linguistic repertoires used.

Exhibit 3.2

Role Systems

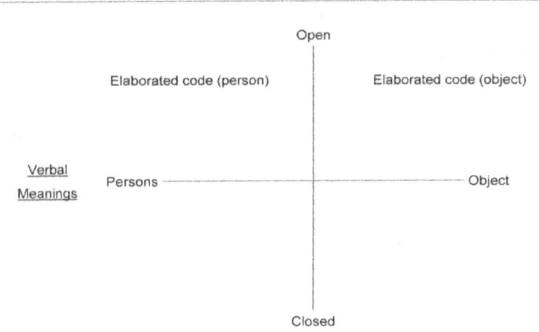

Open

Elaborated code (person)   Elaborated code (object)

Verbal
Meanings   Persons ———————————————————— Object

Closed

Bernstein's Causal Connection Between Role Systems, Communication Codes, and the
Realization of Different Orders of Meaning and Relevance

Bernstein's Causal Connection Between Role Systems,
Communication Codes, and the Realization of Different Orders of
Meaning and Relevance

Situations also involve different role relationships that
result from a number of factors, including membership in
different professional associations, difference in education
levels and fluency , and difference in economic and social
positions. These role relationships in turn determine either
an elaborated communication code if the role system is
open or a restricted communication code if the system is

111

closed. In essence the sociolinguistic thesis implies the existence of different linguistic repertories as a result of the different social role relationships. For example, various professional affiliations create different linguistic repertoires or codes for intragroup communications and/or intergroup communications which lead to a differential understanding of social realtoinships.[37] Specifically, a select set of accounting concepts was subjected to analysis using multidimensional scaling techniques to evaluate the intergroup perceptual differences between three groups of users. A sociolinguistic construct was used to justify the possible lack of consensus on the meaning of accounting concepts. The dimensions of the common perceptual space were identified and labeled as conjunctive, relational, and disjunctive by analogy to the process of concept formation. The sociolinguistic thesis was verified for both the conjunctive and the disjunctive concepts.

The Bilingual Thesis

The best tests of the Sapir-Whorf hypothesis can be provided by bilinguals as they are the only ones who can personally testify to the different *Weltanschauungs* created by different languages. There are various expressions of the differential effect of the worldview imposed by different languages. Consider the following statement: "Language is so intimately interwoven with the whole of social behavior that a bilingual, for better or worse, is bound to differ from the monoglot.[38]

But bilingualism is not the only situation that may result in different worldviews created by different languages. Diglossia is another case. Diglossia occurs when a society uses two or more languages for intrasociety

communication. It is basically manifested by the existence of stable and separable communication codes that
depend on each other but serve different social functions.
Basically some societies rely on separate dialects or functionally differentiated language varieties.[39] Fishman, in
fact, makes the separation between high (H) language,
used in conjunction with religion, education, and other
aspects of high culture, and low (L) language used in
conjunction with everyday aspects of society.[40] Charles
A. Ferguson, who introduced the concept of diglossia,
perceived H and L as superposed language.[41] Fishman
distinguishes several different kinds of linguistic relationships between H and L languages as follows:

1. H is classical and L is vernacular, the two being
   genetically related, as in classical and vernacular
   Arabic, classical and classicized Greek (Katarevusa)
   and Demotiki, to name only a few.
2. H is classical and L is vernacular, the two not being
   genetically unrelated, as in Loshn Koydesh (textual
   Hebrew/Aramaic) and Yiddish.
3. H is written/formal spoken and L is vernacular, the
   two being genetically related to each other, as in
   Spanish and Guarani in Paraguay.
4. H is written/formal and L is vernacular, the two
   being genetically related to each other, as in High
   German and Swiss German.[42]

The important fact is that different social roles and
relationships dictate the use of different languages or
dialects resulting in different worldviews and attitudes:

Where one set of behaviors, attitudes and values supported, and was expressed in, one language, another set of behaviors, attitudes and values supported and was expressed in the other. Both sets of behaviors, attitudes and values were fully accepted as culturally legitimate and complementary (i.e. nonconfictual) and indeed, little if any conflict between them was possible in view of the functional separation between them.[43]

Both bilingualism and diglossia have an impact on the use of language. Speakers of multiple languages or different dialects will experience different worldviews in their use of languages from unilinguals. Different languages or dialect systems may provide cognitive enrichment or linguistic and perceptual confusion. Switching from one language or dialect to another may lead to better perception. In effect, language switching has been found to be related to higher levels of creativity and cognitive feasibility,[44] concept formation,[45] verbal intelligence,[46] and psycholinguistic abilities.[47] The three problems identified can affect the perception of accounting concepts by bilingual and unilingual speakers of languages or dialects. Janice Monti-Belkaoui and Ahmed Belkaoui conducted an experiment to evaluate the extent of these problems in accounting.[48] The findings supported the contention that unilingual speakers of separate languages differ from each other and from bilingual speakers in their perception of concepts. Some of these findings also provided support for the contention that language switching may enhance understanding. The evidence suggests that fluency in more than one language aids in the uniform acquisition and comprehension of concepts.

Linguistic Relativism: A Model

A phenomenon may be represented as language-based given the existence of the two components of symbolic representations and grammatical characteristics. The judgment/decision process is determined by the impact of language on behavior and attitudes as hypothesized by the linguistic relativity hypothesis, the sociolinguistic hypothesis, and the bilingual thesis. Basically the linguistic codifiability or structure of language affects the linguistic and nonlinguistic behavior of users. The social roles created by different professional memberships, social classes, and education lead to different communication codes, either elaborated or restricted, that affect concept formation, understanding, and decision making. Finally, the use of different languages or dialects, as in bilingualism or diglossia, provides speakers with a different understanding of a phenomena as well as different cognitive abilities. The three results contribute to a linguistic relativism model, as portrayed in Exhibit 3.3, which is assumed to determine the judgment/decision process.

Conclusion

The essence of linguistic relativism is the presence of a linguistic process that is assumed to guide the judgment/decision process. The model in this chapter postulates that a phenomenon as a language-based affects the judgment/decision process as result of the theory and findings underlying the Sapir-Whorf hypothesis of linguistic relativity, the sociolinguistic thesis, and the bilingualism or diglossia thesis.

Exhibit 3.3

Linguistic Relativism: A Model

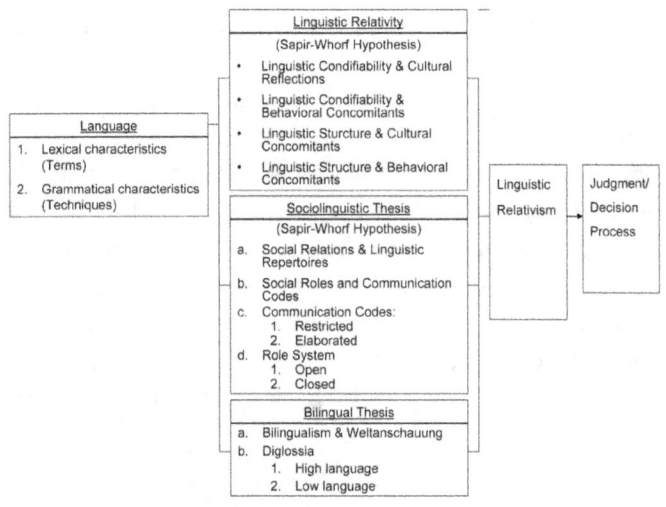

Notes

1. E. Sapir, in D. G. Mandelbaum, ed., *Culture, Language and Personality: Selected Essays,* (Cambridge, Mass.: MIT Press, 1956).

2. B. L. Whorf, *Language, Thought and Reality* (Boston: MIT Press, 1951).

3. Ibid., 214.

4. Ibid., 212.

5. Ibid., 84-85.

6. E. Sapir, "The Status of Linguistics as a Science," *Language* 5 (1929): 207-14.

7. B. L. Whorf, "Science and Linguistics," *Technological Review* 44 (1940): 229-31, 247, 248.

8. Ibid., 212.

9. J. A. Fishman, *The Sociology of Language* (New York: Newbury House, 1972), 156.

10. Roger Brown, "Reference: In Memorial Tribute to Eric Lenneberg," *Cognition* 4 (1976): 125-53.

11. Ibid., 128.

12. Paul Kay and Willett Kempton, "What Is the Sapir-Whorf Hypothesis?" *American Anthropologist* 86 (1984): 66.

13. J. A. Fishman, "A Systematization of the Whorfian Hypothesis," *Behavioral Science* 5/4 (1960): 332.

14. Ibid.

15. R. Linderman, *Der Begriff Der Conscience in Franzosichen Den ken* (Leipzig: Jena, 1938).

16. R. D. Gastil, "Relative Linguistic Determinism," *Anthropological Linguistics* 1/9 (1959): 24-38.

17. Ibid., 37.

18. J. B. Carroll and T. S. Casagrande, "The Function of Language Classification in Behavior," in E. E. Maccoby, T. M. Newcomb, and E. L. Hartley, eds., *Readings in Social Psychology* (New York: Holt, Rinehart and Winston, 1958), 13.

19. R. W. Brown and E. H. Lenneberg, "A Study in Language and Cognition," *Journal of Abnormal and Social Psychology* 49 (1954): 454-62.

20. E. H. Lenneberg, "Cognition in Ethnolinguistics," *Language* 29 (1953): 463-71.

21. E. H. Lenneberg, "A Probabilistic Approach to Language Learning," *Behavioral Science* 2 (1957): 1-12.

22. De Lee Lantz and Volney Steffbre, "Language and Cognition Revisited," *Journal of Abnormal and Social Psychology* 2 (1953): 454-62.

23. Whorf, "Science and Linguistics," 247.

24. G. L. Trager, "The Systematization of the Whorf Hypothesis," *Anthropological Linguistics* 1 (1959): 31-35.

25. Whorf, "Science and Linguistics,"

26. H. Hoijer, "Cultural Implications of the Navaho Linguistic Categories," *Language* 27 (1951): 111-20.

27. Susan Erwin-Tripp, "Sociolinguistics," in L. Berkowitz, ed., *Advances in Experimental Social Psychology* (New York: Academic Press, 1969), 91-163.

28. J. B. Carroll and T. S. Casagrande, "Function of Language Classification in Behavior."

29. Ibid.

30. Basil Bernstein, "A Sociolinguistic Approach to Socialization, with Some Reference to Educability," in John J. Gumperz and Dell Hymes, eds., *Directions in Sociolinguistics: The Ethnography of Communication* (New York: Holt, Rinehart and Winston, 1972), 472.

31. Susan M. Erwin-Tripp, "An Analysis of the Interaction of Language, Topic and Listener," *American Anthropologist* 66/6 (1964): 86-102.

32. Erwin-Tripp, "Sociolinguistics," 91-165.

33. John J. Grumperz, "Linguistic and Social Interaction in Two Communities," *American Anthropologist* 66/6 (1964): 137-54.

34. Dell Hynes, "Modes of the Interaction of Language and Social Setting," *Journal of social Issues* 23/2 (1967): 8-28.

35. Bernstein, "Sociolinguistic Approach to Socialization with Some Reference to Educability," 474.

36. Ibid., 478-79.

37. Ahmed Belkaoui, "The Interprofessional Linguistic Communication of Accounting Concepts: An Experiment in Sociolinguistics," *Journal of Accounting Research* (Fall 1980): 362-74.

38. Robert H. Lowe, "A Case of Bilingualism." *World* 1 (1945): 249-59.

39. J. A. Fishman, "Bilingualism with and without Diglossia; Diglossia with or without Bilingualism," *Journal of Social Issues* 2 (1967): 29-39.

40. Ibid., p. 30.

41. Charles A. Ferguson, "Diglossia," *World* 15 (1959):325-40.

42. J. A. Fishman, "Bilingualism and Biculturalism, as Individual and Social Phenomena," *Journal of Multilingual and Multicultural Development* 1 (1980): 3-15.

43. Fishman, "Bilingualism with and without Diglossia; Diglossia with or without Bilingualism," 29-30.

44. E. Peal and W. E. Lambert, "The Relationship of Bilingualism to Intelligence," *Psychological Monographs* 1 (1962): 76-84W. W. Liedke and L. D. Nelson, "Concept Formation and Bilingualism," *Alberta Journal of Educational Research* 2 (1968): 4-20.

45. W. E. Lambert, and G. R. Tucker, "The Benefits of Bilingualism," *Alberta Journal of Educational Research* (Sept. 1973): 115-22.

46. M. C. Casserby and A. P. Edwards, *Detrimental Effects of Grade One Bilingualism Programs: An Exploratory Study,* paper presented at the annual conference of the Canadian Psychological Association (Toronto 1979).

47. Janice Monti-Belkaoui and Ahmed Belkaoui, "Bilingualism and the Perception of Professional Concepts," *Journal of Psycholinguistic Research* 12/2 (1983): 111-27.

References

Belkaoui, Ahmed. "The Impact of Socio-Economic Accounting Statements on the Investment Decision: An Empirical Study." *Accounting, Organizations and Society* (Sept. 1980): 263-83.

————. "The Interprofessional Linguistic Communication of Accounting Concepts. An Experiment in Sociolinguistics." *Journal of Accounting Research* (Fall 1980): 362-74.

————. "Linguistic Relativity in Accounting." *Accounting, Organizations and Society* (Oct. 1978): 97-124.

Bernstein, Basil. "A Sociolinguistic Approach to Socialization, with Some Reference to Educability." In *Directions in Sociolinguistics: The Ethnography of Communication,* edited by John J. Gumperz and Dell Hymes, p. 472. New York: Holt, Rinehart and Winston, 1972.

Brown, Roger. "Reference: In Memorial Tribute to Eric Lenneberg." *Cognition* 4 (1976): 125-53.

Brown, R. W., and E. H. Lenneberg. "A Study in Language and Cognition." *Journal of Abnormal and Social Psychology* 49 (1954): 454-62.

Carroll, J. B., and T. S. Casagrande, "The Function of Language Classification in Behavior." In *Readings in Social Psychology,* edited by E. E. Maccoby, T. M. Newcomb, and E. L. Hartley. New York: Holt, Rinehart and Winston, 1958.

Casserby, M. C., and A. P. Edwards. *Detrimental Effects of Grade One Bilingualism Programs: An Exploratory Study.* Paper presented at the annual conference of the Canadian Psychological Association. (Toronto 1979).

Erwin-Tripp, Susan. "Sociolinguistics." In *Advances in Experimental Social Psychology,* edited by L. Berkowitz, pp. 91-165. New York: Academic Press, 1969.

‒‒‒‒. "An Analysis of the Interaction of Language, Topic and Listener." *American Anthropologist* 66/6 (1964): 86-102.

Ferguson, Charles A. "Diglossia." *World* 15 (1959): 325-40.

Fishman, J. A. "Bilingualism and Biculturalism, as Individual and Social Phenomena." *Journal of Multilingual and Multicultural Development* I (1980): 3-15.

‒‒‒‒. *The Sociology of Language.* New York: Newbury House, 1972.

‒‒‒‒. "Bilingualism with and without Diglossia; Diglossia with or without Bilingualism." *Journal of Social Issues* 2 (1967): 29-39.

‒‒‒‒. "A Systematization of the Whorfian Hypothesis." *Behavioral Science* 5/4 (1960): 332.

Gastil, R. D. "Relative Linguistic Determinism." *Anthropological Linguistics* 1/9 (1959): 24-38.

Grumperz, John J. "Linguistic and Social Interaction in Two Communities." *American Anthropologist* 66/6 (1964): 137-54.

Hawes, Leonard C. *Pragmatics of Analoguing.* Reading, Mass.: Additon-Wesley, 1975.

Hoijer, H. "Cultural Implications of the Navaho Linguistic Categories." *Language* 27 (1951): 111-20.

Hynes, Dell. "Modes of the Interaction of Language and Social Setting." *Journal of Social Issues* 23/2 (1967): 8-28.

Ijiri, Yuji. *Theory of Accounting Measurement.* Studies in Accounting Research No. 10. Sarasota, Fla.: American Accounting Association, 1975.

Kay, Paul, and Willett Kempton. "What Is the Sapir-Whorf Hypothesis?" *American Anthropologist* 86 (1984): 66.

Lambert, W. E., and G. R. Tucker. "The Benefits of Bilingualism." *Alberta Journal of Educational Research* (Sept. 1973): 115-22.

Lantz, De Lee, and Volney Stefbre. "Language and Cognition Revisited." *Journal of Abnormal and Social Psychology* 2 (1953): 454-62.

Lenneberg, E. H. "Cognition in Ethnolinguistics." *Language* 29 (1953): 463-71.

———. "A Probabilistic Approach to Language Learning." *Behavioral Science* 2 (1957): 1-12.

Liedke, W. W., and L. D. Nelson. "Concept Formation and Bilingualism." *Alberta Journal of Educational Research* 2 (1968): 4-20.

Linderman, R. *Der Begriff Der Conscience in Franzosichen Den ken.* Leipzig: Jena, 1938.

Lowie, Robert H. "A Case of Bilingualism." *World* 1 (1945): 249-59.

McDonald, Daniel. *Comparative Accounting Theory.* Reading, Mass.: Addison-Wesley, 1972.

Monti-Belkaoui, Janice, and Ahmed Belkaoui. "Bilingualism and the Perception of Professional Concepts." *Journal of Psycholinguistic Research* 12/2 (1983): 111-27.

Peal, E., and W. E. Lambert. "The Relationship of Bilingualism to Intelligence." *Psychological Monographs* 1 (1962): 76-84.

Sapir, E. *Culture, Language and Personality: Selected Essays,* edited by D. G. Mandelbaum. Cambridge, Mass.: MIT Press, 1956.

———. "The Status of Linguistics as a Science," *Language* 5 (1929): 207-14.

Trager, G. L. "The Systematization of the Whorf Hypothesis." *Anthropological Linguistics* 1 (1959): 31-35.

Whorf, B. L. *Language, Thought and Reality.* Boston: MIT Press, 1951.

———. "Science and Linguistics." *Technological Review* 44 (1940): 229-31, 247, 248.

Zaltman, Gerald, C. R. A. Pison, and R. Angelman. *Metatheory and Consumer Research.* New York: Holt, Rinehart and Winston, 1973.

Organizational Culture Relativism

Introduction

The reaction of individuals working in different firms to a given phenomenon differs. The reason for this difference is the organizational culture unique to each firm. The organizational culture relativism model in this chapter postulates that various organizational phenomena and characteristics create a distinct corporate culture in each firm that influences and/or dictates the judgment/decision process.

Organizational Culture Relativism: A Model

The efficiency of a corporate culture requires the development of a general paradigm that helps members determine what is in the best interests of the corporation.

The paradigm provides members with a sort of master routine that enables them to solve two related problems stemming from the boundedness of their rationality. The first problem is they, as individuals, are limited in their ability to comprehend and process information. The paradigm may give them categories, processing routines, and examples of good and bad solutions, that will greatly increase their ability to determine how to operate in the class....

[The paradigm] may provide shared frameworks, language, and referents that can help members start from similar assumptions in deriving solutions to previously unfamiliar problems.[1]

The corporate culture paradigm gives the individual faced with a phenomenon categories, processing routines, and schemes that helps solve problems in the best interest of the culture. This is in essence an organizational culture relativism thesis that states that organizational culture through shared frameworks, languages, and reflections determines the judgment/decision process in accounting. The model, as illustrated in Exhibit 4.1, postulates that various organizational factors, including metaphors, symbolisms, internalization, modes of governing transactions, and type of executive personality affect both the processes of organizational commitment and organizational socialization in such a way as to create a specific cooperate culture, which in turn determines the judgment/decision process of individuals faced with a phenomenon.

Underlying Assumptions and Metaphors of Organization

Various metaphors or images have been used to illustrate the type of experience generally referred to as an "organization." This is a result of the tendency of scientists to create knowledge about the world by examining the effects of different metaphoric categorizations of their subjects.[2] Organizations, for example, have been viewed, using metaphors from the physical world, as organism and machine.[3] Other metaphors include "theaters" for performance of roles, dramas, and scripts,[4,5] and "political arenas," aimed at the pursuit and display of power.[6,7]

Exhibit 4.1

Organizational Culture Relativism

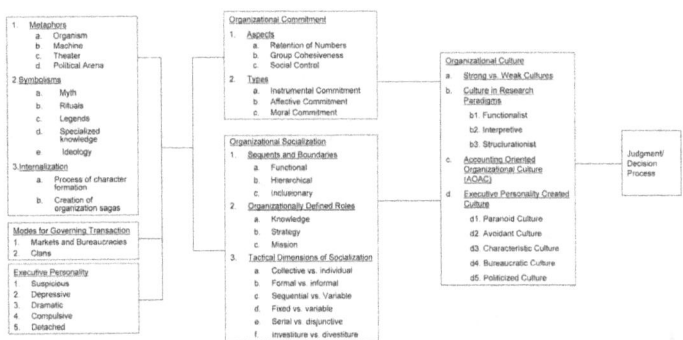

Underlying these metaphors is the presence of a culture that expresses the values or social ideals and the beliefs that organizational members come to share. The manifestation of these values or patterns of beliefs is in the form of symbolic devices such as myths,[8] rituals,[9] legends,[10,11] and specialized language.[12] These symbolisms constitute aspects of the more cultural and expressive components of organizational life.[13] They are internalized either through a process of character formation (an embodiment of values in an organizational structure through statements of mission, program of activity, selective recruitment, and specialization)[14] or the creation of organizational sagas (a system of collective understanding of unique accomplishment in a formally established group).[15]

In the context of our model, the metaphors, the values held by the members of the organization, the symbolisms adopted, the process of character formation, and the creation of organizational sagas affect and determine the type of organizational socialization and commitment processes adopted.

Models for Governing Transactions

W. G. Ouchi proposed three alternative modes for governing exchanges or transactions: markets, bureaucracies, and clans.[16] They are explicated as follows.

A market form of governance uses the price mechanism in competitive situations as a mode of governing exchanges and as an efficient mechanism of control. Contracts between parties are made at a "fair price," insuring a perception of equity among self-interested parties bounded by a given rationale. Those conditions are not, however, always prevalent.

Under conditions of increased ambiguity (a unique product of rapidly changing environmental conditions), however, the bounded rationality of parties makes transactions more costly because the parties have difficulty writing a sufficiently detailed and prescient contract to insure the equitable assessment of value and prohibit self-interested individuals from taking unfair advantage of the ambiguity. Under such conditions, markets may fail.[17]

Bureaucracies as a form of governance under conditions of ambiguity rely upon a mixture of close evaluation with a socialized acceptance of common objectives and the creation of incomplete contracts in the form of employment contracts. While markets rely on prices, bureaucracies rely on rules. This creates important differences.

In any case, rules differ from prices in the important sense that they are partial rather than complete handles of information. A price implies that a comparison has taken place, a comparison between alternative buyers or sellers of the value of the object in question. A rule, however, is essentially an arbitrary standard against which a comparison is yet to be made. In order to use a rule (e.g., a budget, or cost standard) a manager must observe some actual performance, assign some value to it, and then compare that assigned value to the rule in order to determine whether the actual performance was satisfactory or not. All this consumes a great deal of administrative overhead. If the rule is expressed qualitatively rather than quantitatively, the cost of administration can be expected to be higher.[18]

As the third mode of governing transactions, clans socialize the parties to the exchange in such a way that though self-interested, they see a common benefit in the exchange and congruence with their objectives. Clans basically rely upon a relatively complete socialization process that effectively eliminates goals in congruence between individuals.

The clan as a governing mechanism is tantamount to the creation of a specific organizational culture. In fact, "the clan requires such a relatively greater degree of social understanding, specific to the organization, about the general objectives, methods, and values of the collective that it clearly may be thought of as control or governance by means of a local culture that is analogous to the paradigmatic anthropological culture."[19]

Conditions conductive to the development of clans include: (1) a long history and a stable membership, allowing one generation of members to pass on knowledge to successive generations, in the process contributing to the institutionalization of social knowledge;[20] (2) the absence of institutional alternatives, given that contradiction may lead to a loss of the sense of taken-for-granted reality;[21] and (3) interactions among members, as a way of encouraging the continued reinforcement and development of shared knowledge about the social world.[22]

In addition to the market, bureaucracy, and clan categories, Max Boisot and John Child introduce the category of fief to take into account other transaction-governance possibilities that may be more consistent with the social preferences emanating from a traditional culture.[23] By focusing on the informational aspect of economic transaction and by differentiating between levels of information condition and diffusion, they propose a taxonomy of four transaction-governance structures (see Exhibit 4.2).[24] This transaction-governance structure employs both uncodified and undiffused information.

One is characterized by transacting with relatively noncodified information that is asymmetrical distributed with the relevant population (i.e., has low diffusion). Historically this mode is exemplified by the fief as a social organization, i.e., small numbers, hierarchically structured through face-to-face and personalized power relationships that often have to be charismatically legitimated by such means as the laying-on of hands, initiation of rites, commendation ceremonies, and the like.[25]

Exhibit 4.2

Typology of Transaction-Governance Structures

Codified Information	2. <u>Bureaucracies</u> — Information diffusion limited and under central control — Relationships impersonal and hierarchical — Submission to super-ordinate goals — Hierarchical coordination — No necessity to share values and beliefs	3. <u>Markets</u> — Information widely diffused, no control — Relationships impersonal and competitive — No superordinate goals-- each one for himself — Horizontal coordination through self-regulation — No necessity to share values and beliefs
Uncodified Information	1. <u>Fiefs</u> — Information diffusion limited by lack of codification to face-to-face relationships — Relationships personal and hierarchical (feudal/charismatic) — Submission to super-ordinate goals — Hierarchical coordination — Necessity to share values and beliefs	4. <u>Clans</u> — Information is diffused, but still limited by lack of codification to face-to-face relationships — Relationships personal but nonhierarchical — Goals are shared through a process of negotiation — Horizontal coordination through negotiation — Necessity to share values and beliefs

Source: Reprinted from "The Iron Law of Fiefs: Bureaucratic Failure and the Problem of Governance in the Chinese Economic Reforms" by Max

In the context of the model shown in Exhibit 4.1, the modes for governing transactions in general and clans and fiefs in particular contribute to the process of organizational commitment and organizational socialization that result ultimately in a distinct organizational culture.

The Executive Personality

Where power is consolidated in the hands of a top executive or a small, homogeneous dominant coalition, there is a potential link between the executive personality and the organizational culture. Where the problem of culture becomes a concern is in firms with relatively dysfunctional, neurotic executives. For example, Kets de Vries, F. R. Manfred, and D. Miller identify five potential neurotic styles, their fantasies, and their impact on organizational culture and the organization.[26]

1. The suspicious style is associated with a fantasy of persecution that leads to a paranoid culture and a paranoid organization. Hypotheses for the paranoid constellation are shown in Exhibit 4.3.
2. The depressive style is associated with a fantasy of helplessness that leads to an avoidant culture and a depressive organization. Hypotheses for the depressive constellation are shown in Exhibit 4.4.
3. The dramatic style is associated with a fantasy of grandiosity that leads to a charismatic culture and

a dramatic organization. Hypotheses for the dramatic style are shown in Exhibit 4.5.

4. The compulsive style is associated with a fantasy of control that leads to a bureaucratic culture and a compulsive organization. Hypotheses for the compulsive style are shown in Exhibit 4.6.

5. The detached style is associated with a fantasy of detachment that leads to a politicized culture and a schizoid organization. Hypotheses for the detached style are shown in Exhibit 4.7.

Exhibit 4.3

Hypotheses for the Paranoid Constellation

1. The persecutory fantasy and the suspicious style will go together.

2. The more pronounced these personality and cultural factors are in the CEO and his/her top managers, the more the organizational culture will be plagued by: suspiciousness and mistrust; the search for and identification of enemies in the environment; poor morale; fight/flight attitudes; uniform but distorted perceptions; and the use of information as a power resource.

3. The more pronounced these personality and cultural factors, the more the structure of the organization will use: sophisticated control and information systems; centralized power for decision making; and a sophisticated scanning apparatus to study the environment.

4. The more pronounced these personality and cultural factors, the more wariness enters into decision making; the more reactive and fragmented the strategy; and the greater the proclivity to diversify.

Source: Manfred F. R. Kets de Vries and Danny Miller, "Personality, Culture and Organization," *Academy of Management Review* (Apr. 1986): 271. Reprinted with permission.

Exhibit 4.4

Hypotheses for the Depressive Constellation

1. The fantasy of helplessness and the depressive (avoidant/dependent) style will be found in the same CEO's.
2. The more pronounced these personality and cultural factors are in the CEO and his/her managers, the more the organizational culture will be characterized by: a lack of initiative; unmotivated absentee executives; buck-passing; delays; "decidophobia"; passivity; and a sense of futility.
3. The more prominent these personality and cultural factors, the more the structure of the firm will be: bureaucratic; rigid; impersonal; and based on formal position (mechanistic). There will be very little scanning of the environment or communication among managers.
4. The more prominent these factors, the more moribund the strategy which will be less likely to have changed materially in a long time, and which will be anachronistic, even in the mature industries in which these firms are usually found. Extreme conservatism, a very vague set of goals and strategies, and an absence of plans will also be more common.

Source: Manfred F. R. Kets de Vries and Danny Miller, "Personality, Culture and Organization," *Academy of Management Review* (Apr. 1986): 272. Reprinted with permission.

Exhibit 4.5

Hypotheses for the Dramatic Constellation

1. The fantasy of grandiosity and the dramatic (histrionic/narcissistic) style will be found in the same personality.

2. The more pronounced these personality and cultural factors are in the CEO and his/her managers, the more the organizational culture will be characterized by dependent subordinates who: idealize the leader; hold him/her infallible; and never question him/her. There will be an enthusiastic adherence to the beliefs and goals of the CEO, and a paucity of independent-minded executives. A charismatic culture will prevail.

3. The more prominent these personality and cultural factors, the more the structure of the organization will be: extremely centralized; too informal for its administrative task; too primitive in its scanning and information processing apparatus; and too constrained in its bottom-up communications.

4. The more prominent these factors, the more intuitive, impulsive, and risky the decision making, and the more proactive, expansionalistic, and acquisitions-oriented the strategy.

Source: Manfred F. R. Kets de Vries and Danny Miller, "Personality, Culture and Organization," *Academy of Management Review* (Apr. 1986): 274. Reprinted with permission.

Exhibit 4.6

Hypotheses for the Compulsive Constellation

1. The fantasy of control will conjoin with the compulsive style.
2. The more pronounced these personality and cultural factors are in the CEO and his/her managers, the more the culture of the organization will center around issues of control. Efficiency or the slavish adherence to an archaic set of standards and the prevalence of risk averse, bureaucracy-loving managers will prevail. Ritual will rule.
3. The more prominent these personality and cultural factors, the more the structure of the organization will be: bureaucratic; hierarchical; rigid; rule-oriented; inwardly focused; formalized; and centralized. Programmed, routinized, and standardized practices will dominate. Cost controls will monitor efficiency but there will be very little analysis of the environment.
4. The more prominent these factors, the more decision making will focus on details and established procedures. A fixed strategy will prevail; this is never questioned but merely "implemented," through action plans, capital budget, etc.

Source: Manfred F. R. Kets de Vries and Danny Miller, "Personality, Culture and Organization," *Academy of Management Review* (Apr. 1986): 276. Reprinted with permission.

Exhibit 4.7

Hypotheses for the Schizoid Constellation

1. The fantasy of detachment will coincide with the detached (schizoid/avoidant) style.
2. The more pronounced these personality and cultural factors are in the CEO, the more the culture of the organization will be characterized by a leadership vacuum, and dominated by a second tier of politicized "gamesmen" who jockey for power and position. Coordination and cooperation will be neglected.
3. The more prominent these personality and cultural factors, the more the structure of the organization will be fragmented into uncooperative "fiefdoms." Political battles will use information systems as power resources and effective communication and collaboration will be thwarted. Power will be distributed among an altering coalition of second tier managers.
4. The more prominent these factors, the more fragmented, vacillating, and inconsistent the strategies. The absence of consensus will make concerted and adaptive change less possible. Politics will be a far more important influence on decisions than rationality; a muddling-through orientation will be common.

Source: Manfred F. R. Kets de Vries and Danny Miller, "Personality, Culture and Organization," *Academy of Management Review* (Apr. 1986): 277. Reprinted with permission.

Where firms are healthy because of a mixture of personality styles, the impact on culture and the organization will be more salutary. In the context of the model shown in Exhibit 4.1, the type of executive personality affects the processes of organizational commitment and socialization to produce a specific corporate culture.

Organizational Commitment

Commitment to a utilitarian organization, in which the sources of control and motivation are material rather than psychological or symbolic, is difficult given that such an organization generally lacks a compelling ideology and is impersonal and rational, involving only segmental portions of the self. In addition, involvement in such an organizaiotn tends to be largely calculative. What, then, leads to commitments in these organizations? Before examining this question, the concept of commitment must be explicated.

Commitment was first viewed as a form of institution-alization, "the integration of the expectations of actors in a relevant interactive system of roles with a shared norma-tive pattern of values."[27] An elaboration of the concept of commitment from norms to other aspects of a social system was provided by R. M. Kantor as follows: "Commitment may be defined as the process through which individual interests become attached to the carrying out of socially organized patterns of behavior which are seen as fulfilling those interests, as expressing the nature and needs of the person."[28] Three major aspects of a social system affect commitment, namely, retention of members, group cohesiveness, and social control.[29]

Retention refers to people's willingness to stay in the system, to continue to staff it and carry out their roles. Group cohesiveness denotes the ability of people to "stick together," to develop the mutual attraction and collective strength to withstand threats to the group's existence. And social control involves the readiness of people to obey the demands of the system, to conform to its values and beliefs and take seriously its dictates.[30]

Commitment involves, then, the desire to stay in the group, to stick with other members, and to abide by the rules, a three-level process involving *instrumental* commitment (commitment to a social role), *affective* commitment (commitment to relationships), and *moral* commitment (commitment to norms and values). In the context of social action theory, the person cognizes, and evaluates.[31] "That is, he orients himself with respect to the rewards and costs that are involved in participating in the system, with respect to this emotional attachment to the people in the system, and with respect to the moral compellingness of the norms and beliefs of the system."[32]

Bruce Buchanan distinguishes between three components of commitment: "(a) identification adoption as one's own the goals and values of the organization, (b) involvement psychological immersion or absorption in the activities of one's work role, and (c) loyalty a feeling of affection for and attachment to the organization."[33]

Various empirical studies have sought to identify the correlates of commitment. First, social involvement with colleagues and personal investments such as length of organizational service, age, and hierarchical position were found to be related to commitment.[34] Second, organization identification was found to be determined by a sense of work accomplishment, relations with supervisors, and length of organizational service.[35] Third, identification with the organization was found to be related to opportunities for personal achievement provided by the organization, access to power within the organization, and absence of competing objects of identification.[36] Finally, role tension, years of organizational service, and dissatisfaction with the bases of organizational advancement were also found to be good predictors of commitment.

In the context of the model shown in Exhibit 4.1, the underlying assumptions and metaphors, the modes of governing transactions, and the type of executive personality affect the process of organizational commitment so as to produce a specific corporate culture.

Organizational Socialization

The organizational socialization process is an attempt by the experienced members of an organization to teach new members their view of the organizational world and its traditions. As defined by John Van Maanen and Edgar H. Scheim, it is the process by which these new individuals learn the social knowledge and skills demanded by their new organizational role, that is, the cultural perspective of the role[37] required for all the moves made in the organization, whether upward, downward, or lateral.

A descriptive conceptual scheme of organizational socialization, proposed by Van Maanen and Scheim, is adopted here. Six assumptions are made: (1) the individual undergoing the organizational transition is in an anxiety-producing situation; (2) the socialization process does not take place in a vacuum; (3) the socialization process is vital to the stability and productivity of the organization; (4) there is great variation in the way people adjust to novel circumstances; (5) individuals, not organizations, create and sustain beliefs; and (6) the descriptive scheme proposed transcends the particular and peculiar and aims for the general and typical.[38]

Organizationally defined roles are assumed to exits, guarded by segments and boundaries. The organizationally defined roles are assumed to assess a content of knowledge base, a strategic base suggesting the ground rules for the choosing of particular solutions, and an explicit/implicit mission, purpose, and mandate. These segments and boundaries are derived from the three dimensions of an organizationally defined role: functional, hierarchical, and inclusionary.[39] The functional dimension or boundary refers to the various tasks performed by members of an organization, including marketing, finance, production, administrative staff, personnel, research, and development. The hierarchical dimension or boundary refers to the distribution of rank within an organization and the definition of responsibilities. The inclusionary dimension or boundary refers to the individual's inclusion within the organization. For the newcomer each of these dimensions represents boundaries to be eventually crossed by submitting to the appropriate organizational socialization process and ultimately becoming an insider. The filtering process differs depending on the type of boundary.

Hierarchical boundaries crossed by persons moving upward are associated usually with filtering processes carrying notions of merit, potential, and judged past performance, although age and length of service are often utilized as surrogate measures of "readiness" to move upward in an organization. Functional boundaries usually filter people on the basis of their demonstrated skill or assumed aptitude to handle a particular task. However, when functional boundaries are relatively permeable, as they often are, the filtering process may operate on the premise that there are people in the organization who "need" or "wish" to broaden their work experiences. Finally, inclusionary filters, in the main, represent evaluations made by others on the scene as to another's "fitness" for membership.[40]

Once barriers are crossed, the new comer reacts to the role either as a caretaker[41] or as an innovator. What leads to the change is the use of a tactic of organizational socialization, which refers to the ways in which the experiences of persons from one role to another are structured for them by others in the organization.[42] Six major tactical dimensions that characterize the structural side of organizational socialization are proposed.[43] They include: (1) *collective* versus *individual socialization processes;* (2) *formal* versus *informal socialization processes;* (3) *sequential* versus *variable socialization processes;* (4) *fixed* versus *variable socialization processes;* (5) *serial* versus *disjunctive socialization processes;* and (6) *investiture* versus *divestiture socialization processes.*

While collective socialization involves the socialization of a group of new members together through a common set of experiences, individual socialization involves the processing of an individual through individual experiences. Formal socialization involves putting the newcomer through a set of experiences specifically tailored for him/her while informal socialization does not differentiate the newcomer from

147

the other organizational members through the use of informal tactics. Sequential socialization involves the use of a given sequence of discrete and identifiable steps leading to a target role while random specialization involves changing the sequence of steps. In fixed socialization, the newcomer is aware of the time required to complete a given passage while in variable socialization, he/she is not provided any clues about when to expect a given boundary passage. In the serial socialization process, the newcomer follows the footsteps of predecessors who serve as role models while in the disjunctive process the newcomer is left on one's own, to perform the heroic myth,"[44] prevalent in Western fairy tales.[45] In the investiture socialization process, the individual is praised for ones personal characteristics while in the investiture socialization process, the person is defined and stripped of the same personal characteristics, a process similar to Goffiman's "total institutions,"[46] with the deliberate "mortifications to self" which entry into them entails.

In the context of our model, the various indentified organizational characteristics affect the process of organizational socialization so as to create a specific corporate culture that will shape the judgment/decision process.

Organizational Culture

The concept of organizational culture or corporate culture has been given various definitions. It was assumed to be embodied and transmitted by "stories," "myths," and "symbols." It was referred to as a set of shared understandings, interpretations, or perspectives that allow members to articulate contextually appropriate accounts.

Stephen R. Barley provided a definition that integrates all these terms:

From the observation that this family of terms is repeatedly associated with the notion of culture, one may infer that in organization studies "culture" is somehow implicitly tied to notions of social cognition and contextual sense making. Whatever else it may be said to be, culture appears to have something to do with the way members of a collective organize their experience.[47]

Basically members of a group develop a system of publicly and collectively accepted meanings, such as terms, forms, categories, and images, that allows them to explain their own situation to themselves,[48] and to symbolically create an ordered world.

Various characterizations of organizational culture are of importance to the model illustrated in Exhibit 4.1.

Attempts have been made to contrast "strong" homogeneous cultures with "weak" heterogeneous cultures that deviate from management philosophy and are assumed to lack integration.[49,50] Katheleen L. Gregory criticized this type of dichotomization, arguing that it would be more accurate to separate cultural integration from organizational integration and to describe organizations rather than cultures as either strong or weak in terms of integration:

Organizations that lack integration may be comprised of members acting from numerous internally consistent but externally conflicting cultures. Ethnocentrism exacerbates the intensity of conflicts, since each coalition takes its position for granted or may even assume meanings and priorities are shared. The cultures may conflict only in a few situations, or in many.[51]

Organizational cultures may be viewed from at least three perspectives.[52,53] The functionalist research paradigm views culture as an organizational variable. The interpretive research paradigm views it as a pattern of symbolic discourse, something the organization is. The structuralist research paradigm views it as a system of integrated subcultures, not as a unified set of values to which all organizational members subscribe.

Organizational cultures may also be accounting-oriented. More specifically, Andrew P. Thomas argued that enterprises can be conceptualized in terms of the extent to which they have an accounting-oriented organizational culture.[54] It is assumed to take the form of a continuum representing the extent to which accounting is used as a symbol,[55,56] a language,[57,58] ideology,[59,60] rituals,[61] myths,[62] and witchcraft, magic, and ceremony.[63]

The analogy follows from Andrew Pettigrew's suggestion that culture has five elements: symbols, language, ideology, rituals, and myths.[64] The accounting-oriented organizational culture is shown by Andrew P. Thomas to have an impact on choices of corporate reporting practices.[65] In the context of our model, the concept of accounting-oriented organizational culture is assumed to depend on the organizational socialization process and to affect the judgment/decision process in accounting.

The neurotic styles of the executive can create a distinct neurotic culture.[66,67] More specifically, the following associations are hypothesized: (1) suspicious style creates a paranoid culture; (2) depressive style creates an avoidant culture; (3) compulsive style creates a bureaucratic culture; (4) dramatic style creates a charismatic culture, and (5) detached style creates a politicized culture.[68]

Conclusion

An efficient organizational culture requires the sharing of frameworks, referents, and languages that shape the schemes individuals use when faced with phenomena. The model in this chapter argues in favor of such relativism whereby the organizational culture ultimately determines the judgment/decision process.

Notes

1. Alan Wilkins and William G. Ouchi, "Efficient Cultures: Exploring the Relationship Between Culture and Organizational Performance," *Administrative Science Quarterly* 28 (1983): 475.

2. .R. H. Brown, *A Poetic for Sociology* (Cambridge: Cambridge University Press, 1977).

3. Gareth Morgan, "Paradigms, Metaphors and Puzzle Solving in Organization Theory," *Administrative Science Quarterly* 25 (1980): 605-22.

4. Erving Goffman, *The Presentation of Self in Everyday Life* (New York: Doubleday, 1959).

5. I. L. Mangham and M. A. Overington, "Dramatism and the Theatrical Metaphor," in M. Gareth, ed., *Beyond Method: Social Research Strategies* (Beverly Hills, Calif.: Sage, 1983), 219-33.

6. Michel Cozier, *The Bureaucratic Phenomenon* (Chicago: University of Chicago Press, 1964).

7. Jeffrey Pfeffer, "Management as Symbolic Action: The Creation and Maintenance of Organizational Paradigms," in Larry L. Cummings and Barry M. Staw, eds., *Research in Organizational Behavior* (Greenwich, Conn.: JAI Press, 1981), 1-52.

8. D. M. Boje, D. B. Fedor, and K. M. Rowland, "Myth Making: A Qualitative Step in OD Interventions," *Journal of Applied Behavioral Science* 18 (1982): 17-28.

9. Terrence E. Deal and Allan A. Kennedy, *Corporate Cultures* (Reading, Mass.: Addison-Wesley, 1982).

10. I. I. Mitroff and R. H. Kilmann, "On Organization Stories: An Approach to the Design and Analysis

of Organizations Through Myths and Stories," in R. H. Kilmann, L. R. Pondy, and D. P. Slevin, eds., *The Management of Organizational Design* (New York: Elsevier, 1976), 183-207.

11. Alan Wilkins and Joanne Martin, "Organizational Legends" (working paper, Graduate School of Business, Stanford University, 1980).

12. John A. Y. Andrews and P. M. Hirsch, "Ambushes, Shootouts, and Knights of the Roundtable: The Language of Corporate Takeovers," in Louis R. Pondy, et al., eds., *Organizational Symbolism* (Greenwich, Conn.: JAI Press, 1982).

13. Andrew M.Pettigrew, "On Studying Organizational Cultures," *Administrative Science Quarterly* (Dec. 1974): 520-81.

14. P. Selznick, *Leadership in Administration* (Evanston, Ill.: Row, Peterson, 1957).

15. Burton R. Clark, "The Organizational Saga in Higher Education," *Administrative Science Quarterly* 17 (1979): 174-84.

16. W. G. Ouchi, "A Conceptual Framework for the Design of Control Mechanisms," *Management Science* (Sept. 1975): 831-47.

17. Alan L. Wilkins and William G. Ouchi, "Efficient Cultures: Exploring the Relationship Between Culture and Organizational Performance," *Administrative Science Quarterly* 28 (1983): 470.

18. Ouchi, "A Conceptual Framework for the Design of Control Mechanisms," 831.

19. Wilkins and Ouchi, "Efficient Cultures," 472.

20. P. L. Berger and T. Luckmann, *The Social Construction of Reality* (Garden City: Anchor Books, 1967).

21. Ibid.

22. Wilkins and Ouchi, "Efficient Cultures," 472-74.

23. Max Boisot and John Child, "The Iron Law of Fiefs: Bureaucratic Failure and the Problem of Governance in the Chinese System Reforms," *Administrative Science Quarterly* 33 (Dec. 1988): 507-27.

24. Ibid., 509.

25. Ibid., 508.

26. Manfred F. R. Kets de Vries and D. Miller, "Personality, Culture, and Organization," *Academy of Management Review* 11 (1986): 266-79.

27. T. Parsons and E. A. Shils, *Toward a General Theory of Action* (New York: Harper and Row, 1962), 20.

28. R. M. Kantor, "Commitment and Social Organization: A Study of Commitment Mechanisms in Utopian Societies," *American Sociological Review* (Aug. 1968): 500.

29. R. M. Kantor, *Commitment and Community* (Cambridge, Mass.: Harvard University Press, 1972), 67.

30. Ibid., 65.

31. Ibid., 68.

32. M. E. Sheldon, "Investments and Involvements as Mechanisms Producing Commitment to the Organization," *Administrative Science Quarterly* 16 (1971): 143-50.

33. Bruce Buchanan, "Building Organizational Commitment: The Socialization of Managers in Work Organizations," *Administrative Science Quarterly* 18 (1974): 533.

34. Sang M. Lee, "An Empirical Analysis of Organizational Identification," *Academy of Management Journal* 14 (1971): 213-26.

35. M. E. Brown, "Identification and Some Conditions of Organizational Involvement," *Administrative Science Quarterly* 14 (1969): 346-55.

36. L. C. Hrebiniak and J. A. Alutto, "Personal and Role-Related Factors in the Development of Organizational Commitment," *Administrative Science Quarterly* 18 (1973): 555-72.

37. John Van Maanen and Edgar H. Schein, "Toward a Theory of Organizational Socialization," in Barry M. Staw, ed., *Research in Organizational Behavior* (Greenwich, Conn.: JAI Press, 1979), 211.

38. Ibid., 215-16.

39. E. H. Schein, "The Individual, the Organization and the Career: A Conceptual Scheme," *Journal of Applied Behavioral Science* 7 (1971): 401-26.

40. Van Maanen and Schein, "Towards a Theory of Organizational Socialization," 224.

41. E. H. Schein, "Occupational Socialization in the Professions: The Case of the Role Innovator," *Journal of Psychiatric Research* (1971): 521-30.

42. John Van Maanen, "People Processing: Major Strategies of Organizational Socialization and Their Consequences," in J. Paap, ed., *New Directions in Human Resource Management* (Englewood Cliffs, N.J.: Prentice-Hall, 1978).

43. Ibid.

44. T. Campbell, *The Hero with a Thousand Faces* (New York: Anchor Books, 1956).

45. B. Bettelheim, *The Uses of Enchantment: The Meaning and Importance of Fairy Tales* (New York: Alfred A. Knopf, 1976).

46. E. Goffman, *Asylums* (New York: Random House, 1961).

47. Stephen R. Barley, "Semiotics and the Study of Occupational and Organizational Cultures," *Administrative Science Quarterly* 28 (1983): 393.

48. Andrew M. Pettigrew, "On Studying Organizational Cultures," *Administrative Science Quarterly* (Dec. 1979): 574.

49. Terrence E. Deal and Allan A. Kennedy, *Corporate Cultures: The Rites and Rituals of Corporate Life* (Reading, Mass.: Addison-Wesley, 1982).

50. Thomas T. Peters and Robert H. Waterman, Jr., *In Search of Excellence* (New York: Harper and Row, 1982).

51. Katheleen L. Gregory, "Native-View Paradigms: Multiple Cultures and Culture Conflicts in Organizations," *Administrative Science Quarterly* 28 (1983): 365.

52. Linda Smircich, "Concepts of Culture and Organizational Analysis," *Administrative Science Quarterly* 28 (1983): 339-58.

53. Patricia Riley, "A Structurationist Account of Political Culture," *Administrative Science Quarterly* 28 (1983): 414-37.

54. Andrew P. Thomas, "The Effects of Organizational Culture on Choices of Accounting Methods" (paper presented at the American Accounting Association annual meeting, Orlando, Fla., 1988).

55. S. Burchell, et al., "The Roles of Accounting in Organization and Society," *Accounting, Organizations and Society* (1980): 5-27.

56. R. J. Boland and L. R. Pondy, "Accounting in Organizations: A Union of Natural and Rational Perspectives," *Accounting, Organizations and Society* 3 (1980): 5-27.

57. D. Cooper, "A Social and Organizational View of Management Accounting," in M. Brownwich and A. G. Hopwood, eds., *Essays in British Accounting Research* (London: Pitman, 1981): 178-205.

58. Ahmed Belkaoui, "Linguistic Relativity in Accounting," *Accounting, Organizations and Society* (Oct. 1978): 97-104.

59. D. Cooper, "Discussion Towards a Political Economy of Accounting," *Accounting, Organizations and Society* 3 (1980): 161-66.

60. D. Cooper and M. J. Sherer, "The Value of Corporate Accounting Reports: Arguments for a Political Economy of Accounting," *Accounting, Organizations and Society* 3 (1984): 207-32.

61. A. Wildavsky, "Economy and Environment/ Rationality and Ritual: A Review Essay," *Accounting, Organizations and Society* (1976): 117-29.

62. R. J. Boland, "Myth and Technology in the American Accounting Profession," *Journal of Management Studies* 19/1 (1982): 109-27.

63. T. E. Gambling. "Magic, Accounting and Morale," *Accounting, Organizations and Society* (1977): 141-51.

64. Pettigrew, "On Studying Organizational Cultures."

65. Thomas, "Effects of Organizational Culture on Choices of Accounting Methods."

66. D. Miller and P. H. Friesen, "Archetypes of Strategy Formulation," *Management V Science* 24 (1978): 921-33.
67. D. Miller and P. H. Friesen, *Organizations: A Quantum View* (Englewood Cliffs, N.J.: Prentice-Hall, 1984).
68. de Vries and Miller, "Personality, Culture, and Organization," 266-79.

References

Andrews, John A. Y., and P. M. Hirsch. "Ambushes, Shootouts, and Knights of the Roundtable: The Language of Corporate Takeovers." In *Organizational Symbolism,* edited by Louis R. Pondy, et al. Greenwich, Conn.: JAI Press, 1982.

Barley, Stephen R. "Semiotics and the Study of Occupational and Organizational Cultures." *Administrative Science Quarterly* 28 (1983): 393.

Belkaoui, Ahmed. "Linguistic Relativity in Accounting." *Accounting, Organizations and Society* (Oct. 1978): 97-104.

Berger, P. L., and T. Luckmann. *The Social Construction of Reality.* Garden City: Anchor Books, 1967.

Bettelheim, B. *The Uses of Enchantment: The Meaning and Importance of Fairy Tales.* New York: Alfred A. Knopf, 1976.

Boisot, Max, and John Child. "The Iron Law of Fiefs: Bureaucractic Failure and the Problem of Governance in the Chinese System Reforms." *Administrative Science Quarterly* (Dec. 1988): 507-27.

Boje, D. M., D. B. Fedor, and K. M. Rowland. "Myth Making: A Qualitative Step in OD Interventions." *Journal of Applied Behavioral Science* 18 (1982):17-28.

Boland, R. J. "Myth and Technology in the American Accounting Profession." *Journal of Management Studies* 19/1 (1982): 109-27.

Boland, R. J., and L. R. Pondy. "Accounting in Organizations: A Union of Natural and Rational Perspectives." *Accounting, Organizations and Society* 3 (1980): 5-27.

Brown, M. E. "Identification and Some Conditions of Organizational Involvement." *Administrative Science Quarterly* 14 (1969): 346-55.

Brown, R. H. *A Poetic for Sociology.* Cambridge: Cambridge University Press, 1977.

Buchanan, Bruce. "Building Organizational Commitment: The Socialization of Managers in Work Organizations." *Administrative Science Quarterly* 18 (1974): 533.

Burchell, S., et al. "The Roles of Accounting in Organization and Society." *Accounting, Organizations and Society* (1980): 5-27.

Campbell, T. *The Hero with a Thousand Faces.* New York: Anchor Books, 1956.

Clark, Burton R. "The Organizational Saga in Higher Education." *Administrative Science Quarterly* 17 (1979): 174-84.

Cooper, D. "A Social and Organizational View of Management Accounting." In *Essays in British Accounting Research,* edited by M. Brownwich and A. G. Hopwood, pp. 178-205. London: pitman, 1981.

―――. "Discussion Towards a Political Economy of Accounting." *Accounting, Organizations and Society* 3 (1980): 161-66.

Cooper, D., and M. J. Sherer. "The Value of Corporate Accounting Reports: Arguments for a Political Economy of Accounting." *Accounting, Organizations and Society* 3 (1984): 207-32.

Cozier, Michel. *The Bureaucratic Phenomenon.* Chicago: University of Chicago Press, 1964.

Deal, Terrence E., and Allan A. Kennedy. *Corporate Cultures: The Rites and Rituals of Corporate Life.* Reading, Mass.: Addison-Wesley, 1982.

De Vries, Manfred F. R. Kets, and Danny Miller, "Personality, Culture, and Organization." *Academy of Management Review* 11 (1986): 266-279.

Etzioni, Amitai. *A Comparative Analysis of Complex Organizations.* New York: Free Press, 1961.

Gambling, T. E. "Magic, Accounting and Morale." *Accounting, Organizations and Society* (1977): 141-51.

Goffman, E. *Asylums.* New York: Random House, 1961.

———. *The Presentation of Self in Everyday Life.* New York: Doubleday, 1959.

Gregory, Katheleen L. "Native-View Paradigms: Multiple Cultures and Culture Conflicts in Organizations." *Administrative Science Quarterly* 28 (1983): 365.

Herbiniak, L. C., and J. A. Alutto. "Personal and Role-Related Factors in the Development of Organizational Commitment." *Administrative Science Quarterly* 18 (1973): 555-72.

Kantor, R. M. *Commitment and Community.* Cambridge, Mass.: Harvard University Press, 1972.

————. "Commitment and Social Organization: A Study of Commitment Mechanisms in Utopian Societies." *American Sociological Review* (Aug. 1968): 500.

Kemberg, O. *Object Relations Theory and Clinical Psychoanalysis.* New York: Aronson, 1976.

Lee, Sang M. "An Empirical Analysis of Organizational Identification." *Academy of Management Journal* 14 (1971): 213-26.

Mangham, I. L., and M. A. Overington. "Dramatism and the Theatrical Metaphor." In *Beyond Method: Social Research Strategies,* edited by M. Gareth, pp. 219-33. Beverly Hills, Calif.: Sage, 1983.

Miller, D., and P. H. Eriesen. *Organizations: A Quantum View.* Englewood Cliffs, N.J.: Prentice-Hall, 1984.

————. "Archetypes of Strategy Formulation." *Management Science* 24 (1978): 921-33.

Mitroff, I. I., and R. H. Kilmann. "On Organization Stories: An Approach to the Design and Analysis of Organizations Through Myths and Stories." In *The Management of Organizational Design,* edited by R. H. Kiomann, L. R. Pondy, and D. P. Slevin, pp. 183-207. New York: Elsevier, 1976.

Morgan, Gareth. "Paradigms, Metaphors and Puzzle Solving in Organization Theory." *Administrative Science Quarterly* 25 (1980): 605-22.

Ouchi, W. G. "A Conceptual Framework for the Design of Control Mechanisms." *Management Science* (Sept. 1975): 831-47.

Parsons, T., and E. A. Shils. *Toward a General Theory of Action.* New York: Harper and Row, 1962.

Peters, Thomas T., and Robert H. Waterman, Jr. *In Search of Excellence.* New York: Harper and Row, 1982.

Pettigrew, Andrew M. "On Studying Organizational Cultures." *Administrative Science Quarterly* (Dec. 1974): 520-81.

Pfeffer, Jeffrey. "Management as Symbolic Action: The Creation and Maintenance of Organizational Paradigms." In *Research in Organizational Behavior,* edited by Larry L. Cummings and Barry M. Staw, pp. 1-52. Greenwich, Conn.: JAI Press, 1981.

Riley, Patricia. "A Structurationist Account of Political Culture." *Administrative Science Quarterly* 28 (1983): 414-37.

Schein, E. H. "The Individual, the Organization and the Career: A Conceptual Scheme." *Journal of Applied Behavioral Science* 7 (1971): 401-26.

―――. "Occupational Socialization in the Professions: The Case of the Role Innovator." *Journal of Psychiatric Research* 8 (1971): 521-30.

Selznick, P. *Leadership in Administration.* Evanston, Ill.: Row, Peterson, 1957.

Sheldon, M. E. "Investments and Involvements as Mechanisms Producing Commitment to the Organization." *Administrative Science Quarterly* 16 (1971): 143-50.

Smircich, Linda. "Concepts of Culture and Organizational Analysis." *Administrative Science Quarterly* 28 (1983): 339-58.

Thomas, Andrew P. "The Effects of Organizational Culture on Choices of Accounting Methods." Paper presented at the American Accounting Association annual meeting. Orlando, Fla., 1988.

Van Maanen, John. "People Processing: Major Strategies of Organizational Socialization and Their Consequences." In *New Directions in Human Resource Management,* edited by J. Paap. Englewood Cliffs, N.J.: Prentice-Hall, 1978.

Van Maanen, John, and Edgar H. Schein. "Toward a Theory of Organizational Socialization." In *Research in Organizational Behavior,* edited by Barry M. Staw, pp. 221, 215-16, 224. Greenwich, Conn.: JAI Press, 1979.

Wildavsky, A. "Economy and Environment/Rationality and Ritual: A Review Essay." *Accounting, Organizations and Society* (1976): 117-29.

Wilkins, Alan, and Joanne Martin. "Organizational Legends." Working paper, Graduate School of Business, Stanford University, 1980.

Wilkins, Alan, and William G. Ouchi. "Efficient Cultures: Exploring the Relationship Between Culture and Organizational Performance." *Administrative Science Quarterly* 28 (1983): 470, 472-75.

Contractual Relativism

Introduction

People in organizations are bound by the covenants and limitations of their employment contracts. Similarly, various financing contracts limit and define the type of financial transactions permissible for a given firm. What these contracts imply in the organization is an effort to monitor the behavior and actions of individuals toward an efficient realization of organizational goals. Therefore, the model in this chapter postulates that the judgment/decision process may be shaped by the permissible behavior and actions defined in the contracts entered by the organization with individuals seeking employment or provision of services.

The Agency Theory: Contractual Views of the Firm

The agency theory was developed in response to the concern about risk sharing, a problem that arises when cooperating parties have different attitudes toward risk.[1,2] Cooperating parties, however, may have different goals and division of labor.[3,4] Organizations are in fact "legal frictions which serve as a nexus for a set of contracting relationships among individuals."[5] Basically contractors or providers of capital (principals) supply the factors of the contracts and the implementation of the work. Therefore, the agency relationship is secured by a contract under which the principal engages the agent to perform some services on his or her behalf. The agency problem arises because the goals of the principal and agent differ and the monitoring of the agent's effort and action is difficult or expensive. The agent, therefore, will not always act in the best interests of the principal. As a result agency costs are incurred. They are equal to the sum of: (1) the monitoring expenditure by the principal, designed to limit the aberrant activities of the agent; (2) the bonding expenditures by the agent to guarantee that he/she will not take certain actions that may be harmful to the principal and to ensure that the principal will be compensated for any losses; (3) the residual loss due to the divergence between the agent's decisions and those decisions which would maximize the welfare of the principal.[6] The focus of agency then becomes the design of an optimal contract between a principal and an agent that are engaged in cooperative behavior, have different goals and attitudes toward risk, and are assumed to be motivated solely by self-interest.

The Stewardship/Accountability Model

Generally, accounting has been viewed as a means of providing the history of an organization and its transactions with its environment. For either the owner or the shareholders of a firm, accounting records provide a history of the manager's stewardship of the owner's resources. The stewardship concept is basically a feature of the principal-agent relationship whereby the agent is assumed to safeguard the resources of the principal and to provide information to the principal on the uses of the resources. The accountability model can be defined as follows:

The primary role of the accountant is to assist the accountor in accounting for his activities and their consequences and, at the same time, provide information to the accountee....[T]he accountability approach...includes not only the traditional stewardship issues centered on the compliance with established rules but also the modern performance issues oriented toward the efficiency and effectiveness notions.[7]

Measurement of the stewardship concept has evolved over time. J. G. Birnberg distinguished four periods: (1) the pure custodial period, (2) the traditional custodial period, (3) the asset-utilization period, and (4) the open-ended period.[8]

The first two periods refer to the need for the agent to return the resources intact to the principal by performing minimal tasks to fulfill the custodial function. In these two periods, the disclosure of the balance sheet data is considered adequate. The third period refers to the need for the agent to provide initiative and insight in using the assets in conformity with agreed-upon plans.

In addition to using the balance sheet, this period requires the acquisition of performance-evaluation data on the effectiveness of the use of the assets. Finally, the open-ended period differs from the asset-utilization period by providing more flexibility in the use of assets and enabling the agent to chart the course of asset utilization. J. C. Birnberg elaborates on this last concept:

This involves not only the initial direction, but also ascertaining the critical point in time when such directions must be changed. Like strategic control, the stewardship function requires that a significant degree of responsibility be assumed by the servant. The task force is probably characterized by a lack of structure and a significant amount of uncertainty. This suggests that we may find our reporting system to the master caught between the rock and hard space of communication the need for the detail on one hand and the risk of overload and excessive complexity on the other.[9]

The stewardship model, in the open-ended period, views the accounting reporting system as a way of mitigating the loss of efficiency produced by the fact that the steward knows more about his actions and the state of the world than the owner, and the conflict of interest caused by the fact that each individual acts in his/her own best interest. The role of the accounting system in mitigating the loss of efficiency is made possible by the strong assumption that the accountant is selfless, honest, and independent.[10]

The Transaction-Cost Economics Model

The transaction-cost economics model attempts to develop a systematic answer to why firms exist, and to explain the circumstances under which hierarchically directed transactions within firms replace market-mediated transactions.

The general approach to economic organization employed here can be summarized compactly as follows: (1) Markets and firms are alternative instruments for completing a related set of transactions; (2) whether a set of transactions ought to be executed across markets or within a firm depends on the relative efficiency of each mode; (3) the cost of writing and executing complex contracts across a market *varies with the characteristics of the human decision makers who are involved with the transactions on the one hand, and the objective properties of the market on the other;* and (4) although the human and environmental factors that impede exchanges between firms (across a market) manifest themselves somewhat differently within the firm, the same set of factors applies to both.[11]

Two human characteristics are assumed to affect this governance choice, namely, bounded rationality and opportunism. Opportunistic behavior is any action used by one party, enjoying an informational (or other) advantage to exploit that advantage to the economic detriment to others. In its crassest form, Williamson uses it to refer to "lying, stealing, and cheating" or other "self-disbelieved statements."[12]

Bounded rationality is the limited computational ability of individuals and their limited ability to acquire and process information. Given the existence of a small number of parties to an exchange, which increases the likelihood of opportunistic behavior, and given the existence of uncertainty/complexity that also increases the likelihood of opportunism, the costs of the transaction are prohibitive and a hierarchy rather than the market would be the best way of carrying forward the transaction. The transaction costs of negotiating, monitoring, harmonizing, and enforcing contracts between two parties are incurred by each. These contracts are, however, assumed to be incomplete as one cannot given the bounded rationality assumption incorporate all contingencies, and courts are to be imperfect enforcers of contracts. Lessening the impact of the incompleteness of contract is an issue, as parties may take advantage of the rise of an unforeseen contingency. The latter behavior is labeled as a hold-up behavior. This situation, characterized by the incompleteness of contracts and self-interested behavior, prevents a cooperative solution from being achieved. How the parties can resolve these problems between themselves (referred to as private ordering) rather than using the courts (referred to as legal ordering) is the question of essence in transaction-cost economics. Governance procedures are devised to achieve the objective of meeting transaction costs arising from the opportunistic behavior caused by the rise of the unforeseen contingencies. One of the opportunistic behaviors most in need of control is the distortion of ex-ante investments in relation-specific assets. More precisely, assets are characterized by a high asset specificity when their use inside the relationship is higher than their use outside the relationship. An opportunistic behavior arises when the same asset is subject to an ex-post hold up behavior.

The Principal-Agent Model

The concern in this model is a general theory of the principal-agent relationship and the derivation of the optimal employment contract within a well-specified model of the agency relationship. Various assumptions are made in the principal-agent model: (1) there is goal conflict between the principal and the agent; (2) the agent is more risk averse than the principal; (3) both agent and principal are rational and have unlimited computational ability; (4) contracts are complete in the sense that first, all contingencies which are verifiable can be used as arguments in the contracts and second, the contracts are accurately enforced by the courts.

Given that the principal cannot determine that the agent has acted well and given their different goals, two agency problems arise generally denoted as moral hazard or hidden action and adverse selection or hidden information.

The moral hazard or hidden action problem refers to the lack of effort exercised by the agent given that effort is a disutility to the agency. The term *moral hazard* originated from the fact that fire insurance dulls incentives for caution and even creates incentives for arson.

The adverse selection or hidden information problem involves a misrepresentation of skill or validity by the agent. It is a case where the agent uses information in making decisions that the principal does not have.

Given the presence of the unobservable behavior due to moral hazard and adverse selection, the principal has two options: either to design an information system that reveals the agent's behavior to the principal or design employment contracts that mitigate the divergence between the cooperative behavior that will maximize the welfare of the individuals and the self-interested behavior that is achievable.

The solution to the basic agency problem consists of:

I) the employment contract, which incorporates:

1. the payment schedule for the agent;
2. the information system choices....;
3. specification of how the agent *promises* to act;

II) the agent's actual action[13]

The optimal choices of these variables and their welfare effects (i.e., risk sharing and production) are the main concern of principal-agent research.

The Positivist Agency Theory

The positivist agency theory explains why certain contractual relationships arise. It describes specifically the governance mechanisms that limit the agent's self-serving behavior in those cases where the principal and the agent are likely to have conflicting goals. For example, M. Jensen and W. H. Meckling showed how increased ownership equity by managers aligns managers' interests with those of the owners.[14] The capital and labor markets are assumed to be efficient and to act as information mechanisms to control the opportunism of top executives.[15]

Similarly, the board of directors is assigned the same information and control roles.[16] In addition, there is evidence in support of agency problems between shareholders and executives across situations in which their interests diverge such as in takeover attempts,[17] debt versus equity financing,[18] and acquisitions and diverstitures.[19] The mitigation of agency problems is shown to be possible through outcome-based contracts such as golden parachutes[20,21] and executive stock holdings,[22] and through information systems such as boards[23] and efficient markets.[24]

Unlike the principal-agent theory, the positivist agency theory assumes that the observed employment and financial contracts are optimal given transaction costs. However, the same transaction costs make the contract incomplete and coupled with the opportunistic behavior of agents make the genesis of cooperation very difficult.

As a result of the above situation, the focus of the positivist agency theory becomes to explain the use of those observed contracts through an examination of the effect that changes in employment and financing contracts have on the behavior of management (i.e., their financing and investment) decisions and on the stock price of the firm.[25]

Design and changes in these contracts may be made through the choice of accounting policies. Positive accounting theory (the Rochester School of Accounting) aims at investigating the economic consequences of voluntary and mandatory choices of accounting techniques and standards.

In general, the prediction of economic consequence theories is driven by contracting and monitoring costs associated with management compensation contracts, bond covenants, regulation, and/or political visibility.[26] These theories assume that changes in the accounting rules used to calculate accounting numbers have economic consequences because they change the distribution of expected cash flows or the claims of various parties to those cash flows. Accordingly, R. L. Watts and J. L. Zimmerman offer the following hypotheses:

Bonus plan hypothesis. Managers of firms with bonus plans are more likely to choose accounting procedures that shift reported earnings from future periods to the current period.[27]

Debt/equity hypothesis. The larger a firm's debt/equity ratio, the more likely the firm's manager is to select accounting procedures that shift reported earnings from future periods to the current period.[28]

Size hypothesis. The larger the firm, the more likely the manager is to choose accounting procedures that defer reported earnings from current to future periods.[29]

Compensation contracts may also be designed to overcome agency problems. This is evidenced by the association between compensation and firm performance,[30-32] positive stock-price reactions to the adoption of golden parachutes,[33] short-term performance plans,[34] and long-term performance plans.[35]

Contractual Relativism

A firm is assumed to be nexus of contracts, whereby contractors or shareholders are suppliers of production factors. The agent coordinates these contracts, initiating and implementing exchanges between shareholders, creditors, employees, customers, and suppliers.

The behavior and action of each of these individuals is assumed to be determined by the specifications of the contract that defines what is permissible and acceptable to the firm. Each of the components of agency theory the stewardship/accountability model, the transaction-cost economics model, the principal-agent model, and the positivist agency model adheres to the notion of the contract that is the guide to permissible behavior and actions in the firm. The situation is also applicable to the individual in the firm faced with the task of providing a solution to a phenomenon. The covenants of the contract defining the relationship between this individual and the firm may provide the necessary guidelines for this individual in dealing with a phenomena. This is the essence of the contractual relativism model, portrayed in Exhibit 5.1. As a result of the assumptions and implications of the four models of agency theory, contracts through their definition of permissible behavior and actions determine the judgment/decision process.

Conclusion

The essence of the model portrayed in this chapter is that contracts define permissible behavior and actions that determine the judgment/decision process. The importance of these contracts results from the assumptions and implications inherent in the four models of agency theory, namely, the stewardship/accountability model, the transaction-cost economics model, the principal-agent model, and the positivist agency model.

Exhibit 5.1

Contractual Relativism: A Model

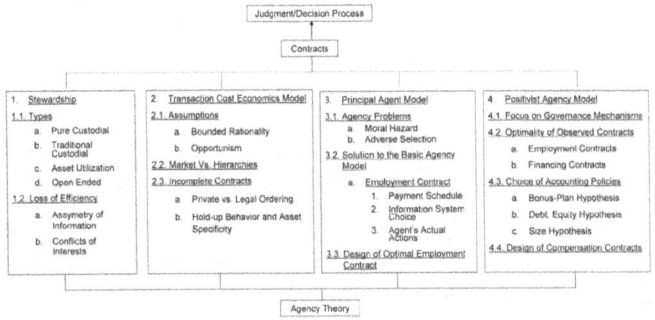

Notes

1. K. Arrow, *Essays in the Theory of Risk Bearing* (Chicago: Markham, 1971).

2. R. Wilson, "On the Theory of Syndicates," *Econometrica* 16 (1968): 119-32.

3. M. Jensen and W. Meckling, "Theory of the Firm: Managerial Behavior, Agency Costs and Ownership Structure," *Journal of Financial Economics* (Oct. 1976): 305-60.

4. S. Ross, "The Economic Theory of Agency: The Principal's Problem," *American Economic Review* 63 (1973): 134-35.

5. Jensen and Meckling, "Theory of the Firm."

6. Ibid., 308.

7. Y. Ijiri, *The Theory of Accounting Measurement,* Studies in Accounting Research No. 10 (Sarasota, Fla.: American Accounting Association, 1975), ix-x.

8. J. C. Birnberg, "The Role of Accounting in Financial Disclosure," *Accounting, Organizations and Society* (June 1980): 73.

9. Ibid., 74.

10. Gjesdal has analyzed the stewardship problem using a principal-agent model. See F. Gjesdal, "Accounting for Stewardship," *Journal of Accounting Research* (Spring 1981): 208-31.

11. O. E. Williamson, *Markets and Hierarchies: Analysis and Antitrust Implications* (New York: Free Press, 1975), 8.

12. Ibid.

13. Stanley Baiman, "Agency Research in Managerial Accounting: A Survey," *Journal of Accounting Literature* (Spring 1982): 154-213.
14. Jensen and Meckling, "Theory of the Firm," 305-60.
15. E. Fama, "Agency Problems and the Theory of the Firm," *Journal of Political Economy* 88 (1980): 288-307.
16. E. Fama and M. Jensen, "Separation of Ownership and Control," *Journal of Law and Economics* 26 (1983): 301-25.
17. R. Walking and M. Long, "Agency Theory, Managerial Welfare and Takeover Bid Resistance," *Rand Journal of Economics* 15 (1984): 54-68.
18. A. Argawal and G. Mandelker, "Managerial Incentives and Corporate Investment and Financing Decision," *Journal of Finance* 42 (1987): 823-37.
19. Y. Amihud and B. Lev, "Risk Reduction as a Managerial Motive for Conglomerate Mergers," *Bell Journal of Economics* 12 (1981): 823-37.
20. H. Singh and F. Hariomto, "Management Brand Relationships, Takeover Risk and the Adoption of Golden Parachutes: An Empirical Investigation," *Academy of Management Journal* (forthcoming).
21. M. Jensen and R. Roeback, "The Market for Corporate Control: Empirical Evidence," *Journal of Financial Economics* 3 (1976): 305-60.
22. Argawal and Mandelker, "Managerial Incentives and Corporate Investment and Financing Decision."
23. R. Kosnik, "Greenmail: A Study in Board Performance in Corporate Governance," *Administrative Science Quarterly* 32 (1987): 163-85.

24. M. Wolfson, "Empirical Evidence of Incentive Problems and Their Mitigation in Ore and Gas Shelter Programs," in J. Pratt and R. Zechhauser, eds., *Principals and Agents: The Structure of Business* (Boston: Harvard Business School Press, 1982), 101-26.

25. Stanley Baiman, "Agency Research in Managerial Accounting: A Second Look" (paper presented at the Inaugural Management Accounting Research conference, School of Accounting, University of New South Wales, Sept. 9-10, 1988, 12).

26. R. W. Holthausen and R. W. Leftuwich, "The Economic Consequences of Accounting Choice: Implications of Costly Contracting and Monitoring," *Journal of Accounting and Economics* (Aug. 1983): 77-118.

27. R. L. Watts and J. L. Zimmerman, *Positive Accounting Theory* (Englewood Cliffs, N.J.: Prentice-Hall, 1986), 208.

28. Ibid., 216.

29. Ibid., 235.

30. Ahmed Belkaoui, "Executive Compensation, Economic Performance, Organizational Effectiveness and Social Performance," *Research in Corporate Social Performance and Policy* (forthcoming).

31. K. Murphy, "Incentives, Learning and Compensation: A Theoretical and Empirical Investigation of Managerial Labor Contracts," *Rand Journal of Economics* (Spring 1986): 59-76.

32. A. Coughlin and R. Schmidt, "Executive Compensation, Management Turnover, and Firm

Performance: An Empirical Investigation," *Journal of Accounting and Economics* (Apr. 1985): 43-66.

33. R. Lambert and D. Larcher, "Golden Parachutes, Executive Decision-Making and Shareholder Wealth," *Journal of Accounting and Economics* (Apr. 1985), 179-204.

34. H. Tehranian and J. Waegelein, "Market Reaction to Short-Term Executive Compensation Plan Adoption," *Journal of Accounting and Economics* (Apr. 1985): 131-45.

35. J. Brickley, S. Bhagat, and R. Lease, "The Impact of Long-Range Management Compensation Plans on Shareholder Wealth," *Journal of Accounting and Economics* (Apr. 1985): 115-30.

References

Amibud, Y., and B. Lev. "Risk Reduction as a Managerial Motive for Conglomerate Mergers," *Bell Journal of Economics* 12 (1981): 823-37.

Argawal, A., and G. Mandelker. "Managerial Incentives and Corporate Investment and Financing Decision." *Journal of Finance* 42 (1987): 823-37.

Arrow, K. *Essays on the Theory of Risk Bearing.* Chicago: Markham, 1971.

Baiman, Stanley. "Agency Research in Managerial Accounting: A Second Look." Paper presented at the Inaugural Management Accounting Research conference, School of Accounting, University of New South Wales, Sept. 9-10, 1988.

———. "Agency Research in Managerial Accounting: A Survey." *Journal of Accounting Literature* (Spring 1982): 154-213.

Belkaoui, Ahmed. "Executive Compensation, Economic Performance, Organizational Effectiveness and Social Performance." *Research in Corporate Social Performance and Policy.* Forthcoming.

Brickley, J. S. Bhagat, and R. Lease. "The Impact of Long-Range Management Compensation Plans on Shareholder Wealth." *Journal of Accounting and Economics* (Apr. 1985): 115-30.

Coughlin, A. and R. Schmidt. "Executive Compensation, Management Turnover, and Firm Performance: An Empirical Investigation." *Journal of Accounting and Economics* (Apr. 1985): 43-66.

Fama, E. "Agency Problems and the Theory of the Firm." *Journal of Political Economy* 88 (1980): 288-307.

Fama, E., and M. Jensen. "Separation of Ownership and Control." *Journal of Law and Economics* 26 (1983): 301-25.

Gjesdal, F. "Accounting for Stewardship," *Journal of Accounting Research* (Spring 1981): 208-31.

Ijiri, Y. *The Theory of Accounting Measurement.* Studies in Accounting Research No. 10. Sarasota, Fla.: American Accounting Association, 1975.

Jensen, M., and R. Roeback. "The Market for Corporate Control: Empirical Evidence." *Journal of Financial Economics* 3 (1976): 305-60.

Jensen, M., and W. H. Meckling. "Theory of the Firm: Managerial Behavior, Agency Costs and Ownership Structure. *Journal of Financial Economics* (Oct. 1976): 305-60.

Kosnik, R. "Greenmail: A Study in Board Performance in Corporate Governance." *Administrative Science Quarterly* 32 (1987): 163-85.

Lambert, R., and D. Larcher. "Golden Parachutes, Executive Decision-Making and Shareholder Wealth." *Journal of Accounting and Economics* (Apr. 1985): 179-204.

Murphy, K. "Incentives, Learning and Compensation: A Theoretical and Empirical Investigation of Managerial Labor Contracts." *Rand Journal of Economics* (Spring 1986): 59-76.

Ross, S. "The Economic Theory of Agency: The Principal's Problem. *American Economic Review* 63 (1973): 134-35.

Singh, H., and F. Hariomto. "Management Brand Relationships, Takeover Risk and the Adoption of Golden Parachutes: An Empirical Investigation." *Academy of Management Journal.* Forthcoming.

Tehranian, H., and J. Waegelein. "Market Reaction to Short-Term Executive Compensation Plan Adoption." *Journal of Accounting and Economics* (Apr. 1985): 131-45.

Walking, R., and M. Long. "Agency Theory, Managerial Welfare and Takeover Bid Resistance." *Rand Journal of Economics* 15 (1984): 54-68.

Williamson, O. E. *Markets and Hierarchies: Analysis and Antitrust Implications.* New York: Free Press, 1975.

Wilson, R. "On the Theory of Syndicates." *Econometrica* 16 (1968): 119-32.

Wolfson, M. "Empirical Evidence of Incentive Problems and Their Mitigation in Ore and Gas Shelter Programs." In *Principals and Agents: The Structure of Business,* edited by J. Pratt and R. Zechhauser, pp. 101-26. Boston: Harvard Business School Press, 1982

Toward A General Judgment Theory

Introduction

The purpose of this chapter is to build on the contributions of the five previous chapters and to suggest a theory to explain and predict the judgment/decision process.

A General Theory

As Exhibit 6.1 shows, the theory explaining the judgment/ decision process is a combinatorial theory. The judgment/ decision process is determined by a cognitive process that is itself altered and uniquely shaped by the particular national culture of the individual faced by the phenomenon (cultural relativism); the particular linguistic repertoire used by the individual (linguistic relativism); the organizational culture of the entity of which the individual considers himself/ herself a dedicated and loyal member (organizational culture relativism); and the covenants and requirements of the contracts binding the individual to a set of norms and allegiances to the firm (contractual relativism).

Exhibit 6.1

A General Theory

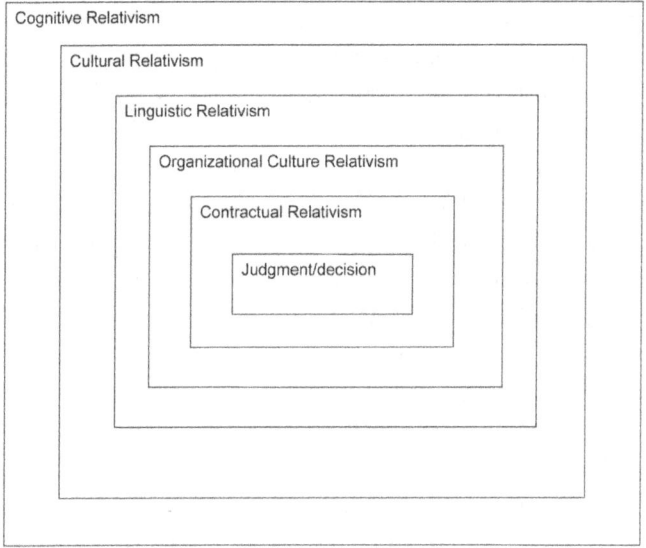

While the cognitive process is viewed as essential in explaining the judgment/decision process, the impact of culture, language, organizational culture, and contracts is assumed to be present in some cases and absent in others. Some factors may be more dominant in some situations than in others. When all the factors are present, the theory postulates that the order of importance of these factors is as follows: cognition, culture, language, organizational culture, and contracts.

Cognitive Relativism

The essence of cognitive relativism is the presence of a cognitive process that is assumed to guide the judgment/decision process. The model outlined in the chapter on cognitive relativism presents the judgment and decision made about a phenomenon as the product of a set of social cognitive operations that includes the observation of information on the phenomenon and the formation of a schema to represent the phenomenon that is stored in memory and later retrieved to allow the formation of a judgment and decision when needed. Therefore, an understanding of the knowledge structures or schemata used by individuals facing a phenomenon is important to an understanding of the judgment/decision process. A similar assessment is made about auditing:

The role of schemata is particularly relevant in auditing, because the schemata developed by auditors through experience and prior knowledge of client situations may affect the manner in which the auditor perceives the evaluation of assertions and the need to accumulate and interpret evidence about these assertions. Thus, understanding the nature of audit expertise may depend on understanding schematic structures, including the differences in complexity of knowledge structures, recall ability, and speed of access among auditors with varying levels of experience. In addition, understanding knowledge structures through descriptive research is essential to the development and validation of expert systems in auditing.[1]

In fact, all phenomena involve the cognitive use of a knowledge structure or schema, developed by individuals through experience, learning, and prior knowledge. For example, D. Frederick characterized a schematic representation of internal control evaluation with respect to transaction cycles.[2] Each transaction cycle (e.g., purchasing and disbursements) was decomposed into a series of functions (e.g., receiving) which were decomposed into a set of specific control procedures (e.g., physical verification of goods received). Each of these knowledge structures and schema shape the manner in which a phenomenon is approached, and guide the judgment/decision process. A schema-driven information search or strategy where the decision maker relies on an experienced-based mental model is assumed to occur when an individual faces a phenomenon.

Cultural Relativism

The essence of cultural relativism is the presence of a cultural process that is assumed to guide the judgment/ decision process. The model as presented in the chapter on cultural relativism postulates that culture through its components, elements, and dimensions dictates the organizational structures adopted, micro-organizational behavior, and the cognitive functioning of individuals faced with a phenomenon. Basically each culture is distinguished from others by thoroughgoing, seemingly fundamental themes. Each culture creates taken-for-granted models of the world that are widely shared by members of the society and which are crucial in their understanding of that world and their behavior in it.[3] Such models are used to perform a variety of different cognitive tasks:

Sometimes, these cultural models serve to set goals for action, sometimes to plan the attainment of said goals, sometimes to direct the actualization of these goals, sometimes to make sense of the actions and fathom the goals of others, and sometimes to produce verbalizations that may play various parts in all these projects as well as in the subsequent interpretations of what has happened.[4]

What may result is that people will comply with certain social behavior because it directly satisfies some culturally defined need, what Spiro called "intrinsic cultural motivation,"[5] or because it realizes some strongly held cultural norm or value, what Spiro called "internalized cultural motivation."[6] Basically, "through the process of socialization individuals come to find achieving culturally prescribed goals and following cultural directives to be motivationally satisfying, and to find not achieving culturally prescribed goals and not following cultural directives to be anxiety producing."[7]

These cultural models represent the schemas that individuals invoke for the performance of such naturally occurring cognitive tasks as categorizing, reasoning, remembering, problem solving, and decision making. In the context of the cognitive relativism model introduced earlier, individuals from different cultures may invoke different knowledge structures or schemas when faced with a phenomenon. Culture plays a central role in the organization of everyday understanding and the retrieval of that information for a judgment/decision process. It implies that knowledge is organized in culturally standardized and hence familiar event sequence, that tells the individual how to react to a particular phenomenon. This point is also acknowledged in cognitive science as "well-developed belief systems about the world."[8]

Linguistic Relativism

The essence of linguistic relativism is the presence of a linguistic process that is assumed to guide the judgment/decision process. The model outlined in the chapter on linguistic relativism postulates that a language-based phenomena affects the judgment/decision process as a result of the theory and findings underlying the Sapir-Whorf hypothesis of linguistic relativity, the sociolinguistic thesis, and the bilingualism or diglossia hypothesis.

The basis of the linguistic relativity hypothesis is that the characteristics of the language, lexical or grammatical characteristics, have a marked influence on the cognitive processes preceding the judgment/decision process. Basically the cognitive organization underlying the development, storage, and retrieval of schemes about phenomena is constrained by the linguistic structure. The degree of fluency and mastery of the language acts as a major determinant in the organization of everyday understanding and the retrieval of that information for a judgment/decision process. It implies that knowledge is organized in linguistically standardized and hence familiar event sequences that tell the individual how to react to a particular phenomenon.

The basis of the sociolinguistic thesis is that different linguistic repertories exist as a result of the different social role relations espoused by individuals facing the phenomena. These different role relationships result from membership in different professional associations, differences in education levels, expertise, and fluency in accounting, and differences in economic and social positions. These role relationships result in the use of either an elaborated communication code if the role system is open or a restricted communication code if the role system is closed. Basically, the nature of the social role held by an individual acts as a major determinant in the organization of everyday understanding and the retrieval of that information for the judgment/decision process. It implies that knowledge is organized as an elaborated or restricted communication code depending on the nature of the social role, that tells the individual how to react to and interpret a phenomenon.

Speakers of different languages or dialects experience different worldviews in their use of languages than unilinguals. The capacity to converse in more than one communication code provides these individuals with different levels of creativity, cognitive feasibility, concept formation, verbal intelligence, and psycholinguistic abilities when faced with a phenomenon. Basically, the mastery of more than one language or more than one dialect acts as a major determinant in the organization of everyday understanding and the retrieval of that information for a judgment/decision process. It implies that knowledge is organized in multilinguistically standardized and hence familiar event sequences that tell an individual how to react to a particular phenomenon in each language.

Organizational Culture Relativism

Organizational cultural efficiency requires the sharing of frameworks, language, and referents that shape the schemata individuals use when faced with a phenomenon. The model outlined in the chapter on organizational culture argues in favor of such relativism whereby the organizational culture to which an individual belongs ultimately determines the judgment/decision process, by providing him/her with schemas of good and bad solutions that will increase the ability to determine how to operate in the organizational culture or clan. Therefore, membership in an organizational culture acts as a major determinant in the organization of everyday understanding of phenomena and the retrieval of that information for a judgment/decision process. It implies that the organizational culture gives the individual faced with a phenomenon categories, processing routines, and schemas that helps solve the problems in the best interests of the culture.

Contractual Relativism

The essence of the model outlined in the chapter on contractual relativism is that contracts define permissible behavior and actions that ultimately determine the judgment/decision process. These contracts may include the blind allegiance to a given faith, creating a religious relativism as a subset of contractual relativism. The importance of these contracts results from the assumptions and implications inherent in the four models of agency theory, namely, the stewardship/accountability model, the transaction-cost economics model, the principal-agent model, and the positivist agency model. Basically the cognitive organization underlying the development, storage, and retrieval of schemas about accounting and/ or auditing phenomena are constrained by the covenants of the contracts entered between individuals and the firm. These covenants act as a major determinant in the organization of everyday understanding and the retrieval of that information in the judgment/decision process.

Conclusion

The theory is based on a cognitive model of judgment/decision process. It states that cognitive process guide the judgment/decision process, and that the schemata underlying this process are in turn shaped by the crucial factors of culture, language, organizational culture, and contractual agreements.

Notes

1. R. H. Ashton, et al., "Audit Decision Making," in *Research Opportunities: The Second Decade* (Sarasota, Fla.: American Accoutning Association 1988), 108-9.

2. D. Frederick, *Auditor's Representations and Retrieval of Knowledge in Internal Control Evaluation* (unpublished doctoral diss., University of Michigan, 1986).

3. N. Quinn and D. Holland, "Culture and Cognition," in D. Holland and N. Quinn, eds., *Cultural Models in Language and Thought* (Cambridge: Cambridge University Press, 1987), 3-40.

4. Ibid., 6-7.

5. M. Spiro, "Social Systems, Personality and Functional Analysis," in B. Kaplan, ed., *Studying Personality Cross-Culturally* (New York: Harper and Row, 1961), 93-177.

6. Ibid.

7. R. D'Andrade, "Cultural Meaning Systems," in R. Shuseder and R. Levine, eds., *Culture Theory: Essays on Mind, Self, and Emotion* (Cambridge: Cambridge University Press, 1984), 88-115.

8. R. Schank and R. Abelson, *Scripts, Plans, Goals and Understanding: An Inquiry into Human Knowledge Structure* (Hillsdale, N.J.: Erbaum, 1977), 132.

References

Ashton, R. H., D. N. Kleinmuntz, J. B. Sullivan, and L. A. Tomassini. "Audit Decision Making." In *Research Opportunities: The Second Decade* (Sarasota, Fla.: American Accounting Association, 1988): 108-9.

D'Andrade, R. "Cultural Meaning Systems." In *Culture Theory: Essays on Mind, Self and Emotion,* edited by R. Schuseder and R. Levine, pp. 88-115. Cambridge: Cambridge University Press, 1984.

Quinn, N. and D. Holland. "Culture and Cognition." In *Cultural Models In Language and Thought,* edited by D. Holland and N. Quinn, pp. 3-40. Cambridge: Cambridge University Press, 1987.

Schank, R. and R. Abelson. *Scripts, Plans, Goals and Understanding: An Inquiry into Human Knowledge Structure.* Hillsdale, N.J.: Erlbaum, 1977, 130-39.

Spiro, M. "Social Systems, Personality and Functional Analysis." In *Studying Personality Cross-Culturally,* edited by B. Kaplan, pp. 93-177. New York: Harper and Row, 1961.

.